THE CHURCH REDEMPTIVE

THE
CHURCH
REDEMPTIVE

Howard Grimes

 ABINGDON PRESS NEW YORK • NASHVILLE

THE CHURCH REDEMPTIVE

Copyright © MCMLVIII by Abingdon Press

Library of Congress Catalog Card Number: 58-7431

Scripture quotations unless otherwise designated
are from the Revised Standard Version of the Bible
and are copyright 1946 and 1952 by the Division of
Christian Education of the National Council of the
Churches of Christ in the U.S.A.

B

SET UP, PRINTED, AND BOUND BY THE
PARTHENON PRESS, AT NASHVILLE,
TENNESSEE, UNITED STATES OF AMERICA

TO MY WIFE

Preface

WHAT I HAVE WRITTEN IN THE FOLLOWING PAGES IS MORE A confession of faith than a reasoned argument: a confession of faith in the importance of the Church in the day-by-day existence of the Christian. Perhaps it may also seem at times unduly critical, for when one talks of the Church as the Body of Christ, or the Fellowship of Believers, or the People of God, or in any of the other terms common to the New Testament, he is thereby bringing judgment on himself and others for our failure to be really that Body, or in the deepest sense The Believers, or in utter seriousness the People of God.

Three central convictions underlie the writing. First, many Protestants have failed to see the significance of the Church as Church and must recover its essential importance and meaning. In America this failure has led to an undue emphasis on the church as a cultural institution, and though the institutional life of the Church neither can nor ought to be ignored, its role in the life of the American church can and should be re-examined and given a less central position.

Second, before the Church can act as the Church, it must understand what it is. Is it really the Body of Christ? the People of God? the Fellowship of the Spirit? any one, or some combination, or all of these, plus many other things? There is wide difference of opinion in the ecumenical church concerning the answer to this question, and the position stated in the first part of the book is a mediating one which seeks to hold in tension various ways of understanding the nature of the Church. All of them, however, point to its essential nature as both of God and of man. Drawing upon the richness of material on the subject, I have tried to state what for me seems to be a Church-theory

7

which holds in dynamic relationship the wealth of meanings and understandings which the New Testament, Church tradition, and modern theological thinking provide for us.

Acting on this conviction, then, I have tried to spell out in general outline what I conceive the work of the Church to be if it is to express its divine nature and mission in the world. In no sense are these last chapters intended to be a blueprint for action. Rather they are thought of as guideposts which must be both modified and tested in a local situation, and discarded insofar as they fail to actualize the life of the Body of Christ in a particular setting. The final chapter in particular attempts to set up criteria for selecting modes of activity in any given situation.

Finally, it is my conviction that out of all these meanings one which is crucial for the life of the contemporary Church is the Church thought of as the *Laos*, the People of God, the Fellowship (*Koinonia*) of men with God and with each other. Therefore, as I have attempted to describe the practical implications of my understanding of the nature of the Church, I have chosen those areas of life and work which directly affect the total membership of the Community as active participants. To be sure, the chapter on worship deals with the functions of the ordained minister as preacher of the Word, leader of worship, and celebrant of the Sacraments. But I have tried to emphasize here, as well as in other sections, the representative character of the ordained ministry and the normative quality of the response of the total congregation. The orientation is always toward the life of the total Body, not the functions of the ordained ministry. Hence the preaching and pastoral offices are almost completely ignored.

Further, my special predilection will no doubt be obvious to the reader: namely, the conviction that the Christian Fellowship must be an agency for nurture and teaching of both the young and the more mature. This is indicated in many ways, but chiefly through an emphasis on the importance of the nurturing of faith through the richness of the interior life of the Fellowship, through pointing out the necessity of transmitting the tradition it bears, and through calling attention to the significance of attempting to evoke a personal response from the individual which involves informed commitment.

My indebtedness to numerous theologians and other authorities has been indicated in the footnotes. My debt to colleagues at Perkins School of Theology, including especially my former fellow teacher in the field of Christian Education, Professor Charles Johnson, is not so easily indicated. Students in classes at Perkins will also be aware that many of these ideas have been tried on them and modified in the process.

Nor is it easy to express my deep appreciation to my wife, Johnnie Marie Grimes, who both acted as a sounding board for many of the ideas and typed the final manuscript.

HOWARD GRIMES

Contents

I

Introduction

"The Church is of God, and will be preserved to the end of time."

"The Church's one foundation is Jesus Christ her Lord."

"On this rock I will build my church, and the powers of death shall not prevail against it."   *(Matt. 16:18b.)*

T HESE THREE STATEMENTS—THE FIRST FROM THE RITUAL FOR church membership of the Methodist Church, the second from a popular hymn written by Samuel Stone in the nineteenth century, and the third from the Gospel of Matthew—affirm the significance of the Church. They assert unmistakably that those who call themselves by the name of Christ cannot do otherwise than take the Church seriously. They remind us further that the Church must be interpreted as more than a human institution, existing for the convenience of and at the whims of human beings. Whatever may be said concerning the obligations placed upon those who have assumed participating membership in the Church, the place to begin in thinking about the nature and mission of the Church is with God who reveals himself in Jesus Christ.

If this be so, then it is appropriate that we should be seriously occupied in the mid-twentieth century with rethinking the nature and mission of the Church. That we are so concerned is illustrated by the fact that such discussions have consumed much of the attention of the World Council of Churches during recent years.[1] Indeed, some observant churchmen feel that the question of the nature of the Church is the most important one now facing ecumenical discussants.

The questions pertaining to the nature and mission of the Church are both "theological" and "practical." Unfortunately these two phases of the discussion are not always brought into dynamic relationship, and the discussions concerned with the *nature* of the Church are not always carried over into the realm of the day-by-day life of the Church in the world. Further, discussions of the *mission* of the Church are often grounded on some unexpressed theology which is inconsistent with the best understanding available of the nature of the Church.

This means, then, that any theologizing about the Church must be carried on on the deepest level possible, that is, in terms of the Church as it expresses itself in the world of men. To use a term which has come into increasing popularity within recent years, these questions must be *existential,* not merely theoretical. It is not enough that we describe and delineate some *ideal* conception of the Church to which we give our assent and then proceed to the realm of action as if such a conception did not exist. Rather, such thinking about what the Church *is* must be concretized in terms of what the Church *does* in Europe, in America, or in some other area of the real world in which we live.

On the other hand, our understanding of the Church cannot be merely pragmatic, that is, involved with its day-by-day existence in the world of men. Surveys of the Church as it now exists in a particular locality, of how it expresses itself in terms of activities, statistics, and institutional acting, are useful but not definitive. We may rejoice in such recent studies as the Blizzard [2] and Niebuhr studies [3] of the ministry, but they are not the final word. Manuals on guiding the life of the local church tend to be oriented primarily toward the elucidation of "how to get and keep members," "how to be a successful leader," "how to get results," in this or that undertaking. Borrowing from the current "how to do it" fads, we are in danger of confusing human accomplishment with God's eternal activity in our world through his Church.

The succeeding pages of this present work are an attempt to relate these two phases of the interior life of the Church: namely, its divine nature and mission and its human character and response. To the end that this may be more clearly understood, early chapters concentrate on its nature as God's primary medium of activity in our world today. In order that the living implications of this theologizing may be seen, the last chapters attempt to indicate some of the directions in which the Church must move in order to act responsibly in our world today.

In order to comprehend the depth of the meaning of the Church as a significant part of God's design for the world, it is first necessary to see the Church as a corporate body—the Body of Christ, to use the Pauline expression. One hesitates to use the phrase "the extension of the incarnation" to decribe the Church; yet if this is understood to signify basically the *body* through which God acts for the redemption of mankind, it is at least permissible if not necessary to indicate the full importance of the Church.

The difficulty of speaking of the Church as the Body of Christ, and especially as the extension of the incarnation, becomes apparent when we recall that the Church is also a covenant community, or the "People of God." God acts in the world through his people; the message of reconciliation is made known through them (II Cor. 5:18-20). A body may easily become a hierarchical institution, as has tended to happen in Roman Catholicism. Thus, we must always see the Church not only as a corporate body, but also as a covenant community, the People of God, the *koinonia* of believers. Jesus Christ is the vine; those who have been joined to him in the Church are the branches (John 15:1-8).

If we take seriously both the reality of the Church as the Body of Christ and its divine mission to be the People of God, we must quickly move on to analyze how the Church expresses its life in the world. Thus in Part II an attempt is made to "spell out" the implications of the Church made alive through Jesus Christ, as the Church alive and acting in the world. Such a Church is first a worshiping community, and secondly a community that nurtures, witnesses, and carries on both its interior life and its witness in the world within the context of its understanding of itself as the redemptive fellowship. In this discussion no attempt is made to indicate all of its means of expression. Those considered are illustrative of some of the major thrusts which, if taken seriously, might lead the Church to be truly the Church in the twentieth century.

In a sense, then, the following pages echo a phrase used by the ecumenical movement a few years back, "Let the Church be the Church." In the day when this expression was current, there was a vague uneasiness on the part of American churchmen that this was a challenge by European churchmen of the "activism" of the American church. And so it was, for often in recent decades the American church has become so concerned with "getting things done" that it has forgotten its nature as the *Body of Christ*. It has too often become primarily an institution of human morality and betterment, not an embodiment ("incarnation") of the Holy Spirit of God. Concurrently, it has tended to capitulate to the trend toward specialization in our age, and its leadership has often taken on the character of professional leaders rather than *ministers* of the gospel of God to human beings.

But the challenge, "Let the Church be the Church," was also aimed at the European church, where inaction sometimes appears to be considered as great a virtue as activity is in the American counterpart. Churches have often been ineffective so far as the daily life of persons is concerned, and the priesthood has often become not a *ministry* set aside to perform certain tasks of guiding and stimulating the laity but rather a hierarchy of those who assume *control* of an institution. Pastor Jean Bosc, writing in reference to Protestantism in France, has summarized this danger effectively.

All our churches suffer from the same evil: clericalism. We can say *grosso modo* that they have become priests' churches: they form in practice a closed spiritual and ecclesiastical domain from which the men who live in the world and struggle with the world's problems are more and more excluded, and in which they feel less and less at home.[4]

Thus, in both Europe and America, the Church must be called back to its original mission, to *be* the Body of Christ in the world, to worship God, to witness to the gospel, and to nurture in its fellowship those who have responded to the call of God in Christ.

If some of the criticism either stated or implicit in the following pages seems unduly harsh, primarily with respect to the American church, let it be remembered they simply point to the gap between the Church as it is and the Church as it might become. For we in America have become enamored by our bigness, our superior organizations, our ability to *get* members, our comfortable ministry, our superior church buildings and parish houses. The outward form too often replaces the inner spirit.

Indeed, the harsh words of Jesus to the scribes and Pharisees may not be inappropriate with respect to the twentieth-century American church:

Woe to you, scribes and Pharisees, hypocrites! for you are like whitewashed tombs, which outwardly appear beautiful, but within they are full of dead men's bones and all uncleanness. So you also outwardly appear righteous to men, but within you are full of hypocrisy and iniquity. (Matt. 23:27-28.)

In all honesty, may we not admit that this is an apt description of the Church as it often exists in twentieth-century America? The words are too harsh, perhaps, but so may we assume that they were with respect to the scribes and Pharisees of the time of Jesus—those keepers of the tradition of Jesus' day. *They* meant well—and so do we. Somehow, however, both they and we have missed the mark, and the manner in which we have done so is strikingly similar. Both we and they are often guilty, to use the words from Second Timothy, of "holding the form of religion but denying the power of it" (3:5*a*). It is easy for us to manifest a conventional, respectable form of Christianity in our churches without manifesting the power of God contained in the gospel for the redemption of mankind, first for those in the Church and then for those outside. (Compare Rom. 1:16.)

Any description of the Church, then, as the Body of Christ, as the medium through which God works, must be set alongside a recognition of the failures and weaknesses of the Church as it is seen in the present time. The Church must be seen both in terms of its actuality and its potentiality, just as any human individual must be so described. The human person is in process of becoming, and so is the Church as it manifests itself in the world.

The amazing story of God's dealing with his human children is that he is able to work in the world in spite of the weaknesses of those to whom he has entrusted the message of reconcilitaion. The remarkable story of Israel—the "Old Israel" in contrast with the "New Israel" or the Church—is the story of God at work in a sinful group, ultimately through this group bringing the light of the gospel to all mankind. To be sure, it was through the dramatic efforts of individuals like Amos, Hosea, Isaiah, Second Isaiah, Jeremiah, and finally Jesus of Nazareth, Son of God and Son of man, that the message of this community was revealed. We must never forget, however, that back of these individuals was always the total community and that it was both *from* and *to* the community that they spoke.

The New Israel of God, like the Old Israel, has often been apostate. Through Augustine and St. Francis and Savonarola and Martin Luther and John Calvin and John Wesley and Karl Barth and Reinhold Niebuhr, God has found new prophets through whom he can speak. Yet all of these were nurtured in the Community of Faith and they spoke both *from* and *to* that Community. So, any modern prophet must first be a part of the Body of Christ before he can speak both from and to that Body as it exists in the world today.

And wonder of wonders: God can use the wrath of men to praise him! This is illustrated pertinently in Paul's dealing with the Christians at Corinth. To them he wrote, "Now you are the body of Christ and individually members of it" (I Cor. 12:27). Yet it was this same community of believers in which there was dissension (1:10), jealousy and strife (3:3, immorality (5:1, 11; 6:9-11), and overeating and drunkenness at the Communion meal (11:21). The Church remains the Church in spite of the apostasy of many of its members, yea, even its leaders.

Thus, the following pages are not intended to be an idealized picture of the Church, but rather a delineation of both what it is and what it is not. For the Church *is* the Body of Christ in spite of its human weaknesses. Its people *are* the People of God in spite of their apostasy. Its fellowship *is* the primary community in which redemption occurs in spite of its shameful inadequacy. Everything that is said about the nature of the Church both exists and does not exist. It exists at least in embryonic form. The bud is there even though the flower may be hidden within the bud.

For like the individual the Church is both redeemed and being redeemed; it exists both in its actuality and in its potentiality. There is always a tension between what it is and what it may become. In a real sense the Church is both dead in its trespasses and alive through Christ Jesus. It is because of this tension that anyone who takes the Church seriously must both exalt it as the Body of Christ and at the same time condemn it for its failure to be in reality the People of God.

This, then, is the Church alive—alive because of God's grace in Christ, potentially alive because of man's response in faith. The words of the Letter to the Ephesians are appropriate in this context:

And you he made alive, when you were dead through the trespasses and sins in which you once walked. . . . God, who is rich in mercy, out of the great love with which he loved us, even when we were dead through our trespasses, made us alive together with Christ (by grace you have been saved). . . . For we are his workmanship, created in Christ Jesus for good works, which God prepared beforehand, that we should walk in them. (2:1-2a, 4-5, 10.)

PART I

THE NATURE OF THE CHURCH

II

The Body of Christ

"Now you are the body of Christ and individually members of it."

(*I Cor.* 12:27.)

THE FIRST ASSERTION THAT MUST BE MADE CONCERNING THE NATURE of the Church is that it is the Body of Christ. This is to proclaim both the divine origin and meaning of the Church. It is to acknowledge that, unlike human institutions, the Church is not primarily of human contriving. To be sure, the Church takes on the *form* of human institutions, and it does work similar to that done by human institutions. It may, in fact, either in terms of its larger human form or as a particular local congregation, cease to be the Body of Christ and become some other type of body. But then it ceases to be the Church. However, we are not capable finally of judging when a particular church group or local congregation has forfeited its right to be called the Body of Christ. We *can* say that only as it retains this original character as the Body of Christ is it really the Church of Jesus Christ.

To state this even more emphatically, it is Christ and not the human members who first constitute the Body. He is the vine, to use the figure from John; we are the branches (15:1-8). But the vine must exist prior to the branches, and the branches wither and die when detached from the vine.

Lest this be conceived in some purely mystical sense, it may be well to illustrate by human counterparts. There is a sense in which any institution, and even a nation, is the lengthened shadow of some person, or persons. The United States of America is, in some ways, the extension of the life and work of George Washington and the others associated with him who brought the nation into being. The Methodist Church, as a separate part of the Christian church, may be

21

said to be an extension of the life of John Wesley; the Church of Scotland and the Presbyterian churches are in a way an extension of the life of John Knox; the Disciples of Christ in a sense are carrying out the life of Alexander Campbell. Insofar as Florence Nightingale is responsible for the beginning of nursing as a separate vocation, the modern expression of care of the sick may be said to be an extension of the life of Florence Nightingale.

In human institutions and practices it is not easy to disavow the past even when a deliberate attempt is made to do so. Modern Russia, for example, has found itself more and more linked to its past as part of the East in spite of a revolution which sought to throw out the past. Because history is a continuous process, it is difficult, if at all possible, to deny its hold either on the individual or on an institution. Further, it is a common practice for both individuals and institutions to glory in their history when any elements of virtue may be found in it.

What is true of human institutions is also true of the Church. The crucial question concerning the Church is not whether Jesus founded it but whether it grew out of the impact of the Word made flesh in human history. That it did is amply attested to by the early documents of the Church, the New Testament. Further, that it has had a continuous history in spite of apostasy, division, and the intrusion of human sin is also evident. Thus observed from the human perspective alone, the Church obviously comes out of history and relives its history in its contemporary setting. Looked at through the eyes of faith, it is the continuation of the life of God that came into the world in Jesus of Nazareth—his Body, an extension of his life in the world through the continued activity of the Holy Spirit.

This view of the Church is broader than any one local church, or one denomination, or any group of denominations. It is larger than the World Council of Churches or any other similar group. Indeed, it may be that there are groups of Christians not usually thought of as a church who are also part of his Body. The Body of Christ is splintered; we can only look forward in faith to the time when it will be reunited. Until that day we may still think of it as a unity even though it actually exists in disunity.

It may be, as some say, that the organized church has so ceased to be truly the Body of Christ that God must choose other media in which his will and way will be expressed in our time. Nothing said in the following pages is intended to imply that God is limited in working through the organized movement called the church. Nor is anything meant to imply that all of the work of the institutional church is God's work. It is the hope, however, that these two may be brought into closer proximity, and that the Church may truly be the Church, the Body of Christ. And it may be that a deeper understanding of the nature and mission of the Church is one way by which this renewal of the Church—which must finally be the work of the Spirit—may be begun.

Contrasting Views of the Church

The view of the Church as a corporate body has not always been accepted, however. At times it has been corrupted into the Roman Catholic version of the Church as the "body of the hierarchy" (that is, a body ruled over by Pope, cardinals, archbishops, bishops, and lesser clergy), while at other times it has been perverted into a view which makes of the Church only a *collection* of individuals. These, according to F. W. Dillistone, may be called, on the one hand, the "imperial" view of the Church, and on the other, the "contractual." In order to understand more fully the nature of the Church as a corporate body, we need to see these two views in contrast with one another.

The imperial, which according to Dillistone has been gaining strength in Roman Catholicism during the past five hundred years, allows little freedom for the individual. There is, in effect, both a totalitarian form of polity and a totalitarian form of religious expression. The thinking of the Roman Catholic priest and layman is increasingly regulated by the institution as more dogma is proclaimed. With Dillistone we can conclude that while "The imperial authority and the universal efficiency of the Roman Church are impressive to an age which seeks for social security and rapid results," nevertheless, "freedom and creativity are values too precious for the continuing life of any society to be sacrificed upon the altar of a smooth-functioning mechanism." [2] Under such a view, the Church becomes the arbiter of life and thought.

It was against such a view of the Church that the Reformation raised its voice of protest, and particularly it was this extreme view that led the sectarian groups to an even more radical rejection of the Church as a corporate body.[3] The fact that Protestantism arose in the age of *laissez-faire* individualism, both in economics and social life in general,

23

was also a factor in this development, of course. Just as the Roman Church of the Middle Ages reflected the feudalism in which it had arisen, so the Protestant churches of the age of democracy and free enterprise reflected the social forces which went into the formation of these aspects of culture. Whatever may have been the multiple causes, however, the fact remains that the view of the Church which became increasingly common in the eighteenth and nineteenth centuries was one which Dillistone calls the *contractual*.

Such a view of the Church has been characteristic in particular of those churches which follow a "congregational type" polity, though it has influenced churches adhering to other forms of polity. Indeed, even the episcopal form of church government has not prevented this theory of the Church from being common in Methodism and to some extent in the Protestant Episcopal Church.[4] This theory, similar to the extreme individualism of *laissez-faire* democracy and quite in harmony with the social contract theory of the origin of all human society, holds that the Church is *nothing more* than a voluntary association of individuals who join themselves together by contract because they have accepted Christ and thus desire to form a church for convenience sake. In the words of John Locke:

A Church I take to be a voluntary society of men joining themselves of their own accord in order to the public worshipping of God in such manner as they judge acceptable to Him, and effectual to the salvation of their souls. . . . I say it is a free and voluntary society. Nobody is born a member of any church; . . . since the joining together of several members into this church-society . . . is absolutely free and spontaneous, it necessarily follows that the right of making its laws can belong to none but the society itself; or at least (which is the same thing) to those whom the society by common consent has authorized thereunto.[5]

It would appear clear that the adherents of this church-theory do not really take the Church seriously. If it is nothing more than a voluntary association of individuals who join themselves together because, presumably, they have had an *individual* religious experience, then it is easy to understand why many people see no particular place for the Church as such, even though they may be attracted to its faith. Further, with such a conception of the Church it is only natural that many persons develop a sense of loyalty to the institution rather than to the Christ whose body the Church is. This view can easily lead to a lack of appreciation of the historic Church, and thus various aberrations in worship, in basic ideas, and in various other aspects of its life may develop.

This extreme individualism no doubt served a useful purpose in breaking the strangle hold of the imperialism of the Roman hierarchy, and it is probably needed in our own day as a corrective to any tendency of the organized church to assume *control* over the thoughts and lives of its individual members. Actually, however, the fear of the Church which accompanied such a view has not prevented the development of elaborate church *organizations*. The writer comes out of a background where organization is probably more than ordinarily complex. The Methodist Church in the United States, with its size, strength, and "connectional" system, may be more prone to complex organization than those churches with a congregational polity. Yet there is considerable evidence that all major communions have recognized some degree of continuity between the separate churches even when maintaining a congregational polity. Thus, the congregational-type local church may become just as top-heavy so far as organization is concerned, even on a national scale, as is the denomination with a more elaborately organized church polity.[6]

Some of the results of our highly organized and interrelated local churches may be far from desirable; yet there is reason to believe that such interrelatedness, however demonic it may become, is nevertheless inevitable from a practical point of view. The Church is *not* just a collection of discrete individuals, each one separate and distinct from the other. Nor is the Church *merely* a local group unrelated to other such groups. The Church becomes some kind of organism, regardless of how much it may fear such a structure. Thus, the attempt to deny, or to minimize, the concept of the Church as the Body of Christ seems inevitably to lead to its becoming some other kind of body, perhaps placing more emphasis on the denominational orientation of the particular group than on its more broadly Christian orientation.

In other words, it is highly improbable that the nature of life itself, being distinctly a social process, makes possible any view of either Church or society which thinks of social groupings as being merely collections of separate parts. Increasingly during recent years our understanding of the nature of life and the relation of the individual to the group makes any such individualism untenable.

25

The Social Nature of the Self

Indeed, the very nature of life itself supports the contention that "no man is an island" unto himself but that such is "a piece of the continent." [7] Modern psychology has rediscovered what has been known by poets and seers all along: namely, the remarkable unity of the human person and the organic unity between individual members. Biblical psychology, as opposed to Greek thinking, also emphasizes the unity of the person, and of persons with one another. The idea of a "soul" separate from the "body" is basically Greek in origin, while the modern psychological understanding of the self as the product of biosocial processes is much more kin to biblical psychology. It is out of this concept of individual unity, of course, that the biblical notion of the resurrection of the dead, not the immortality of the soul, emerges.

Not only must the individual self be conceived in unitary terms; the entire human family is by its very nature related. Paul states this simply in I Cor. 15:22: "For as in Adam all die, so also in Christ shall all be made alive." Modern psychologists are almost one in their recognition of the community nature of the life process. Indeed, the danger in modern psychology is some form of psychic determinism, in which human freedom is obscured in the recognition of the interdependence of human persons. It is only when an additional dimension to life is recognized that human freedom is understood, that dimension being the God-man relationship. The human "I" is confronted not only by other human "thou's" but also by the divine "Thou." The "thou" who is my neighbor calls out the "I" who is potentially myself, but only when the "I" who is myself sees itself standing before the "Thou" who is the author of life and the redeemer of myself is freedom possible.[8]

The blood family illustrates this community nature of life most adequately. Every human child is born of two human parents, and he must be nurtured either in his real family or in a substitute family. From these human relationships—the "I" of the child confronted by the "thou's" in his communities—the *human* self emerges. God has so ordered life that the infant is only a potential self until that which God intends him to be is called forth by other persons in his "field." The human self emerges out of the biological or substitute family. The self is a gift of God both through the biological process of birth and through the sociological process of human society.

26

Now note how this same simple fact exists with regard to the emergence of the self in its relationship to God. As numerous writers have shown, but none so simply and yet so effectively as Reuel Howe,[9] the child's first response to God must be through his parents or substitute parents. In fact, they probably serve as his earliest god. Through them grace, mercy, forgiveness, as well as judgment, discipline, punishment, must be mediated. The child experiences human forgiveness and thus the basis for a later response to God's grace is laid. Verbalization *about* the experience of forgiveness (theologizing) follows the actual experience itself. When adolescent rebellion occurs, parents must be willing to release their children from the worship which they are likely to give to the parents prior to adolescence. All of this is part of the process by which human relationships form the basis for the self-disclosure of the divine Self.

What we have been concerned with has to do with the living experience of faith, which, we have said, originates in relationships. *My* love for my child prepares the way for his knowing *God's* love. This is more basic than verbalizations about the gospel; yet such verbalization does occur. And how do they occur? Paul expressed this fact in these words: "But how are men to call upon him in whom they have not believed? And how are they to believe in him of whom they have not heard? And how are they to hear without a preacher?" (Rom. 10:14.) It is obvious that in the history of the Church God has used persons to make known his saving truth, in relationships, deeds, *and* words. Indeed, this is part of the meaning of the incarnation —*God gave himself* in Christ Jesus. So must we give ourselves to others that the gospel may be proclaimed.

In fact, the work of Christian evangelism, nurture, and teaching is founded on the concept of the responsibility of the individual's witnessing to the Community's message, *not merely his own.* In other words, before I can respond to the gospel there must be a Church, though it is conceivable that this Church might consist of myself and one other and be without institutional form. The normal process by which the gospel is made known is for one person who has been touched by a community of persons whose lives have been transformed by the gospel to reach out to another person and draw him into the Christian community. This process is in keeping with the way in which the human self emerges in the first place.

It should be emphasized that this assertion of the social nature of the self does not deny individual freedom and responsibility. Nor does a view of the Church which recognizes its social nature ignore the individual within the Church. As we shall see in more detail, this is not an either/or matter. This polarity can be seen more clearly as we turn to a more detailed analysis of two other theories of the Church.

The Church as Organism

Having rejected both extremes in our thinking about the Church—namely, the Church as an imperialistic body and the Church as a contract entered into by separate individuals—we must now seek to understand how it may be thought of in some real sense as a Body without denying the responsibility placed upon those who are engrafted into the body.

This tension may be best described in the words from Paul which have already been quoted, "Now you are the body of Christ and individually members of it" (I Cor. 12:27), or in the words of Rom. 12:5, "So we, though many, are one body in Christ, and individually members one of another." It is similarly expressed in Eph. 4: "There is one body," and Christ is the head "from whom the whole body, joined and knit together by every joint with which it is supplied, when each part is working properly, makes bodily growth and upbuilds itself in love" (4:4, 16).[10] These statements make clear that the unity of the Church rests in Christ; on the other hand, they indicate specifically that there are individual members, or individual parts, each of which fulfills a specific purpose.

Because of this need to hold in proper balance the elements of truth found in both of these points of view, we need a Church theory which sees the two in tension with one another. Such a picture of the Church must recognize both the organic nature of the Church and the individual's responsibility within the organism. Dillistone does this through his insistence that the "organic" theory, which is in the direction of the imperialistic but not identical with it, and the "covenantal," in the direction of the contractual but not the same, must be seen as two aspects of the same reality.[11] The Church is the Body of Christ; each of us is individually a member of that body.

In other words the Church is both a *unity* and a *community of persons*. Its unity lies in its faith in Christ (Eph. 4:3-6). Discussions of the World Council of Churches have asserted over and over again that our unity is in Christ; our divisions are human deviations. Just as this is true on the ecumenical level, so is it true for a denomination or a local church. The development of unity is not our business—this already exists through our commitment to the lordship of Christ. The development of *community is* our responsibility, a community which recognizes individual differences but which is rooted and grounded in the unity which is in Christ. Again this may be said concerning the world-wide Church, or it may be said with respect to any separate denomination or local church. The problem is only multiplied when it involves the barriers which divide denominations.

Let us look first at the organic nature of the Church. We may assert at the beginning that individuals, in a real sense, are born into the Body of Christ, that they are engrafted into that Body through baptism (I Cor. 12:13, Rom. 11:17-20, Gal. 3:27), or adopted into Christ, whose Body the Church is (Gal. 4:5, Rom. 8:23). In churches practicing infant baptism this is symbolized and effected through the reception by the Church of the child through baptism before the child can for himself accept the conditions of the covenant.

This, in fact, is the heart of the meaning of infant baptism: it is the beginning of something which is continued until death, for the child must later accept for himself the conditions of the covenant and participate regularly in the Lord's Supper.[12] Perhaps the Protestant Episcopal Church is correct when it has the sponsors of the child, who represent the Church as the Body of Christ, assume the vows of responsibility for the nurturing of the child. The obligation of Christian parents for the Christian nurture of the child is established by the fact that the child is born physically into a Christian family. The obligation of the Church is established by the fact that the child is born by water into the Body of the Church. In neither case does the child ask to be born: he is just born and accepted. Just as the human family exists partly for the reception of the child who is born by the union of man and wife, so the Church exists partly for the purpose of receiving into its fellowship those who cannot yet assume responsibility for themselves.

Since the Church does exist for the purpose of nurturing the child, it has a peculiar responsibility to lead the child who has been received through baptism to commitment and faith when he reaches what we have vaguely called the "age of accountability."[13] Though it cannot force commitment upon him, it can encourage him toward decision. Thus in baptism we symbolize God's acceptance of us through his love and forgiveness. This is the Church "acting out" atonement and justification through faith. Similarly, in confirmation decision through faith and commitment are symbolized. We cannot be sure that genuine decision has occurred; what happens is that man's part in responding to God's initiative is dramatized before the congregation as the vows of the covenant are assumed. The Body of Christ accepts the child through baptism because of its own faith in God; the child later confirms for himself the act of faith previously made on his behalf.

For churches not practicing infant baptism, this acceptance is symbolized in other ways. For example, no church is more opposed to infant baptism than the Baptist groups, especially those churches composing the Southern Baptist Convention. Yet the churches of this convention have done remarkable work in making real the Church's acceptance of the child through their educational programs. Children are accepted into the fellowship even though they have no organic connection with the fellowship until they themselves accept baptism and enter into the covenant relationship of membership.

This, then, is the Church as a living organism, prior to any individual, holding its being because of its relationship to Christ, in a real sense an extension of the incarnation however enmeshed in human sin it may be and however desperately it may be in need of redemption. "The Church is of God, and will be preserved to the end of time . . . All, of every age and station, stand in need of the means of grace which it alone supplies." [14]

The Church as Covenant Community

To stop with this emphasis on the organic nature of the Church is to end ultimately with the imperialistic view of the Church, for it can easily cease being the Body of Christ and become the body of the hierarchy. Paul, it will be remembered, not only said, "You are the body of Christ"; he also said, "and individually members of it" (I Cor. 12:27). He also wrote:

But now the righteousness of God has been manifested apart from law, although the law and the prophets bear witness to it, the righteousness of God through faith in Jesus Christ *for all who believe.* For there is no distinction; since all have sinned and fall short of the glory of God, they are *justified by his grace* as a gift, through the redemption which is in Christ Jesus, whom God put forward as an expiation by his blood, *to be received by faith.* (Rom. 3:21-25a; italics mine.)

30

Here, as in the briefer quotation from First Corinthians, the two sides of redemption are delineated: men are justified (redeemed) by the gift of God's forgiveness (symbolized, we have said, through baptism), but they must believe and accept redemption through Christ by faith. It should be noted that Paul is not an extreme individualist in Romans, though some passages might so indicate, for his figure of the engrafting of the branches in Rom. 11:17-20 argues against any complete individualism. It is equally true, however, that Paul is set against any doctrine of the Church which makes it the determiner of salvation. Faith comes *out of* the community and is *nourished* by the community, but in the final analysis it is the gift of God *through the community to the individual* and must be accepted individually.

Thus Dillistone's counteremphasis is demanded by experience and supported by the New Testament: each person individually must enter into the covenant on which the Church is founded. This for churches practicing infant baptism is through confirmation: the person himself assumes the conditions of the covenant which formerly have been assumed for him by parents, sponsors, Sunday school teachers, pastors, and others in the Church.

The problem, of course, is that this covenantal view is always in danger of slipping over to the contractual, just as the organic is in danger of becoming the imperialistic. Unless those churches which emphasize the covenant constantly remind themselves that the Church is more than a collection of individuals, this is likely to happen. Perhaps the heart of the matter is found in the insistence that the Church is in some manner the way in which God acts. God takes the first step; the Church becomes the means through which this grace is made known. The Church accepts, the individual ratifies; God forgives, man accepts God's forgiveness.

Organism and Covenant Community

What we have implied is that these two views of the Church are needed as corrective of each other. The two must be held in tension.

Again we turn to Dillistone for an illustration of how these two principles can be held together, using the family as the basis of the illustration. Every person is born into a human family and that family, however broken it may be, is an organic unity because of biological necessity. If the family is held together by nothing more than biological ties, it is a defective family and the child is not really accepted.

31

But if the family is in any sense a true community, the child is accepted for what he is. In other words the first movement is from the family to the child. He must be accepted and cared for before he in any sense can accept his share of family responsibility. He is born into an organic unity and, if he is to survive, he must be accepted by that organism.

But this is only half the story. Even though the child is accepted, he may never become a creative member of the family. He may reject family standards, traditions, even the love of his parents, when he reaches the age when he can begin to accept responsibility. There are many prodigal sons who never act as dramatically as the Prodigal Son of the parable in denying their family heritage. In other words the child must enter into a kind of covenant with the family, or else he becomes a prodigal. It is significant, however, that he does remain a prodigal *son*.

The different personalities which constitute the family constantly encounter one another, sometimes in tension, sometimes in deepening fellowship. The life of the family is not simply a smooth unfolding of an inherent biological pattern. There are inevitably tensions. On the other hand there are still deeper reconciliations. An adjustment here, an act of comprehension there, a renunciation, a sharing of another's joy—in direct relation with one another the members of the family can grow in character, in insight, in purposefulness, in charity. Thus through the constant interplay of the organic and the covenantal principles there comes into existence a growing "togetherness" as well as a developing freedom, a unity in diversity, a fulfilment of the destiny of the individual within the framework of the corporate whole. This is the ideal, however far it may exceed the normal standard of attainment.[15]

It is easy to see how these same principles apply to the Church. To quote Dillistone again:

The Church is the Body of Christ: the Church is also the people of the New Covenant. The Church is a Sacramental Organism: it is also a Federal Organization. The Church is the social organism of the Divine Logos manifested in time: the Church is also the covenantal community of the Divine Redeemer constituted through His Cross.[16]

To phrase it somewhat differently, the Church is a gift of God, bestowed upon us because of his grace; yet each of us must appropriate this gift through faith. It is a unity into which we are accepted through no merit of our own; it is a community where those who are accepted pledge their faith each to the other because of their common faith in the God and Father of our Lord Jesus Christ. Or as T. W. Manson has written:

It [the Church] is part and parcel of Christianity itself. Somehow we have to maintain both sides of the paradox: that the Church is the Body of Christ, a living, growing organism, born when He was born; and that the Church is the community of the redeemed, whose redemption is purchased by the death of Christ and appropriated by the faith of the believer.[17]

One additional quotation, from Emil Brunner, also points toward this dual nature of the Church:

It is idle to ask which comes first, the egg or the hen, for both points of view are true. But the question whether the word of Christ or faith comes first admits of no discussion, for faith is the response to the word of Christ. This word is entrusted to the keeping of the Christian fellowship, not, however, as an abstraction, but as the Word of the living Christ, who abides in the fellowship through the Spirit. Therefore the fellowship of Jesus precedes the individual believer as the *mater omnium piorum*. Only by taking this insight seriously can we transcend both Protestant individualism and Catholic collectivism. For the Church is neither a *numerus electorum*, a totality of believers, nor is it a sacred institution, but it is the Body of Christ, consisting of nothing but persons: of Him who is the Head and of those who are members of His Body.[18]

This point has been developed at some length because it is fundamental for the more "practical" considerations to be made later. Unless the life of the Church is carried on with a keen sense of its divine nature, that life may easily become secularized and the Church may become only a society for human betterment. Further, this view seems to be that which is most likely to bridge the gap between churches holding to congregational polity and those believing in the episcopacy in any form. A congregationalist can take the Church seriously without accepting a form of church government which appears to him to lead to imperialism, while a member of a church holding to some "connectional" view can take the idea of the individual covenant in all seriousness without denying the significance of the Church as an organic body.

It should be added that this view of the Church is not offered as a compromise doctrine, however; rather it is suggested that the two views, each in itself legitimate and true to one part of the New Testament, must be held in tension. Both of these emphases are necessary if we are to understand that the "Church is of God, and will be preserved to the end of time . . ." [19] and at the same time "a congregation of faithful men," [20] *"a company of men having the form and seeking the power of godliness, united in order to pray together, to receive the word of exhortation, and to watch over one another in love, that they may help each other to work out their salvation."* [21]

This is another way of saying what we shall be repeating in various ways throughout the subsequent pages of this work: namely, that we cannot of ourselves make the Church. We cannot educate, or create fellowship, or convert anyone, or manipulate the Good Society into being. This is God's work. The Church is finally his gift to us. Yet we must act responsibly. We *are* the individual parts who must respond in such a manner as to become a medium through whom he works. We are witnesses, agents, media, through whom he acts, but it is God who works in us. So it is with the Church: it is the Body of Christ; yet we are individually responsible. No view of the Church seems adequate which does not in some manner hold these two perspectives in proper relationship.

III

The People of God

"But you are a chosen race, a royal priesthood, a holy nation, God's own people."

(I Pet. 2:9.)

IN OUR ATTEMPT TO UNDERSTAND THE NATURE OF THE CHURCH, WE have said first that its origin is with Jesus Christ and that it must be thought of as his Body. It is he who has called it into being, and it is he who sustains it through the activity of the Holy Spirit. Such a view seems consistent both with the New Testament conception of the Church and with our current understanding of the nature of the relationship of the individual to the group.

As we have also seen, however, it is not enough that we look at the Church as a living, growing organism; we must also hold in tension with this view one which considers it as a community of persons. To fail to see it as an organism which owes its existence to Christ as its head is ultimately to view it as a human institution, consisting of a collection of individuals. On the other hand, to fail to take seriously its nature as a community of persons who have entered personally into a covenant with its Lord and Master is to risk making of it a kind of superhuman cult for which we bear no responsibility. To do so would be to deny the significance of the human response in faith to which the New Testament so clearly points.

With this background, then, we are ready to consider one of the cardinal principles of the Reformation: the rediscovery, especially by Martin Luther, of the Church as the "people of God." The more familiar manner of describing this concept is the "priesthood of believers." As part of our understanding of the nature of the Church, especially relevant to the practical matters to be dealt with later, it is essential that we see the Church as a community of believers, all called to serve God. Within the context of such a view, the essential difference in laity and priesthood is overcome, and all—the *laos,* or people of God—are seen as a unity. No single doctrine in Protestant thinking about the Church has more practical implications than this.

Israel as the People of God

In order to understand the meaning of universal priesthood, it is necessary to go back to the Old Testament and examine the Hebrew concept of God's special call to Israel. Indeed, in our thinking in general about the Church, it is necessary for us to see it as, in a real sense, a continuation of the Old Israel. As Robert M. Brown has said in his inimitable way:

So it is never enough to say, "Back to the Reformation," or even "Back to the New Testament." We must go "Back to Abraham." We could even say, "Back to the Garden of Eden," and from there, "Back to God." This would at least locate the foundation of the Church where it belongs—in God rather than man.[1]

As he has also reminded us, an anonymous poem must be set alongside that written by Housman:

How odd	But not so odd
Of God	As those who choose
To choose	The Jewish God
The Jews.	And spurn the Jews.
—Housman	—Anonymous[2]

This assertion, of course, is not meant to minimize the genuinely unique element which entered into the world in the new covenant through Jesus Christ. It is to insist, however, that we must not miss the first acts of the drama of God's redemption—those he performed through Israel—if we are to understand those acts which occurred, or will occur, through the Church. This drama is variously described, but it contains at least the following "acts": creation, covenant (with Israel), Christ, the Church, and the consummation.[3] In other words, the God who acts in Christ is the same God who acted in creation and in our fathers, Abraham, Moses, and the prophets. We cannot understand who we are as Christians except as we see that the God who is now acting through the Church and will act through the consummation is the God who has also acted in the past. Thus we are part of a long drama, with God as the principal actor and Christ as the central historical figure. "In Him all things hold together." (Col. 1:17*b*.)

In this drama of redemption, then, the concept of Israel as the people of God is significant. The self-consciousness of the Hebrew people as chosen of Yahweh is too much a part of the Old Testament to need amplification. In the original covenant it is made quite clear that it is the *whole* people, not a selected part, who are to be God's chosen.

And Moses went up to God, and the Lord called him out of the mountain, saying, "Thus you shall say to the house of Jacob, and tell the people of Israel: You have seen what I did to the Egyptians, and how I bore you on eagles' wings and brought you to myself. Now therefore, if you will obey my voice and keep my covenant, you shall be my own possession among all peoples; for all the earth is mine, and you shall be to me a kingdom of priests and a holy nation. These are the words which you shall speak to the children of Israel." (Exod. 19:3-6.)

The significant words for our discussion are these: "you shall be to me a kingdom of priests and a holy nation." *All* the people are called for special mission.

Unfortunately, as the record of the Old Testament repeatedly shows, the people generally thought of this election as granting special privileges. Yet the prophets repeatedly called the people back to a recognition of the fact that it was not to special privilege but rather to particular responsibility that they were called:

Hear this word that the Lord has spoken against you, O people of Israel, against the whole family which I brought up out of the land of Egypt:

> "You only have I known
> of all the families of the earth;
> Therefore I will punish you
> for all your iniquities." (Amos 3:1-2.)

This idea of special responsibility reached its climax in the words of the postexilic writer in the book of Isaiah:

> Thus says God, the Lord,
> who created the heavens and stretched them out,
> who spread forth the earth and what comes from it,

who gives breath to the people upon it
and spirit to those who walk in it:
"I am the Lord, I have called you in righteousness,
I have taken you by the hand and kept you;
I have given you as a covenant to the people,
a light to the nations,
to open the eyes that are blind,
to bring out the prisoners from the dungeon,
from the prison those who sit in darkness." (42:5-7.)

The Ekklēsia

This sense of divine mission, so characteristic of Israel, was accepted by the early Christians as theirs by virtue of the new revelation which had occurred in Jesus Christ. It is not necessary here to discuss the many ramifications of the doctrine of "election" which are associated with this sense of mission. Whatever else may be said concerning it, it is clear that election is fundamentally a way of viewing the manner in which God has already dealt with his people. Most of our problems over the matter arise when we become involved either in attempting to separate the elect from the nonelect, or when we grow interested in predicting the future. When this happens, we are involved not with the doctrine of election but rather with predestination as it pertains to the future.

This sense of being the people of God, both in the Old Israel and in the New, always grows out of a deep sense of unworthiness. In our moments of deepest insight we know that it is not we who have found God but God who has found us. Surely, then, it is God who *chooses* us, not we who *choose* God! Thereby we acknowledge his call, or election, of us. As G. Ernest Wright has so well stated it:

The doctrine of the Chosen People arose as the natural explanation of a historical fact. Israel as an oppressed minority group in Egypt was marvelously delivered, led through a bleak, inhospitable wilderness, and given a land in which to dwell. That was a simple fact. The Israelite reasoned from fact and event in the light of his knowledge of God. Moses was a remarkable leader, but it was Yahweh who had chosen him and overcome his hesitancy. To the Israelite it was nothing short of miraculous that a great Divine Lord should so take pity on this people, should be so interested in an oppressed minority group, that he should engage in a fateful struggle with Pharaoh, the greatest temporal power of the day, and emerge the victor for their cause. These events were the conclusive proof, not only of God's power and might, but also of his gracious concern for Israel.[4]

The significance of this concept may be seen when we recall that the word most often used for *Church* in the New Testament, *ekklēsia,* means "those who are summoned." The Greek word *ekklēsia* actually referred to a convened assembly. The similar Hebrew word, *qâhâl,* referred to God's people called together. "A 'congregation' is a company of people 'who have come together'; a *quahal* or an *ekklēsia* is a body of people 'who have been called together.' The two original words, Hebrew and Greek, put all the emphasis on the action of God." [5]

In essence, therefore, the Church, the *ekklēsia,* is a body of people, not so much assembling because they have chosen to come together, but assembling because God has called them to Himself; not so much assembling to share their own thoughts and opinions, but assembling to listen to the voice of God.[6]

From this perspective, then, the Church exists wherever persons have been called to be the People of God, or to continue the symbol of the Body of Christ, whenever they have been called into that Body. The call, as the Old Testament prophets make clear, is not one to special privilege but rather to mission. Those who have accepted the summons are engrafted into the living organism—the "vine"—and they become the branches on which the fruit grows.

The Priesthood of Believers

It is against the setting which has just been presented that an understanding of the concept of the universal priesthood of all believers must be sought. This doctrine, so important for Martin Luther, has been largely ignored until, within recent years, it has again come into its own. The specific reference on which it is based is I Pet. 2:9-10:

But you are a chosen race, a royal priesthood, a holy nation, God's own people, that you may declare the wonderful deeds of him who called you out of darkness into his marvelous light. Once you were no people but now you are God's people; once you had not received mercy but now you have received mercy.

Three misunderstandings of this important concept must be noted. The first is the temptation of democracy-minded modern man to identify it with democratic church government, or with a lack of authority in the Church. It does seem logical that it would lead to some kind of universal participation in the Church by all or a majority of its members, and it argues against the concept of centralized despotic authority. Yet it must be seen as much more than this. To identify it with a particular form of church government is especially unfortunate, and even to equate it with "group participation" is to miss the point, even though it does have implications in this direction.

The second misunderstanding is the tendency to interpret the priesthood of believers as meaning simply that there is no need to go through a priest in order to reach God. There *is* this implication in a previous verse, to be sure: ". . . to offer spiritual sacrifices acceptable to God through Jesus Christ" (I Pet. 2:5*b*). But as McNeill has pointed out, the priesthood of all Christians was for Luther a mutual priesthood, not merely a personal one, and Luther seems consistent with the New Testament. "Its reference," McNeill writes, "is not to individual privilege, but to social duty and social experience. It is not self-regarding, but other-regarding. It binds the individual to the group under inviolable obligations of love and service." [7] Further, the "lay priesthood is exercised socially and mutually, never atomically." [8] "Like living stones be yourselves built into a spiritual house, to be a holy priesthood." (I Pet. 2:5.) "You are a chosen race, a royal priesthood . . . that you may declare the wonderful deeds of him who called you out of darkness into his marvelous light." (I Pet. 2:9.) This is to say what has been previously asserted: namely, that God's call does not so much grant special privilege as to exact peculiar responsibility.

A third misunderstanding, or perhaps a difficulty of interpretation, concerns the place of authority of the spiritual leader. Again as McNeill has shown, the priesthood of the few (that is, the ordained) continues, "but in a functional and representative form. The official priesthood is now a ministry, and a summation and representation of the priesthood of all, which is bestowed by Christ." [9] Or as Luther himself put it:

Every one first has to be a Christian and a born priest before he becomes a preacher or a bishop, and neither can pope nor any man make him a priest. But when he is born a priest through baptism, then afterwards comes the office and distinguishes him from other Christians. [10]

40

In other words the concept of universal priesthood does not deny the authority of the minister chosen for a particular office when such authority has been given to that office by the Church. It is true that the practical results of the assertion of lay perogatives have sometimes led to a failure to recognize the *office* of the ordained ministry. In such cases the ordained minister may become little more than a functionary to run the errands of the congregation. Certainly Luther would never have countenanced such a lack of respect for ordination! Anticlericalism has at times been as serious a threat to the well-being of the Church as priestly domination. We have seen the resurgence of such a threat in our time, especially among the extreme right wing of Protestantism. Various groups and individuals, disagreeing on social and economic questions with clergymen, have sought to discredit these clergymen, and often by implication the total ministry, by the aspersions made in the direction of the ordained clergy.

We must recognize, then, that there is an authority of experience and training which must be acknowledged in the trained ministry, just as the Church in the time of Paul recognized the apostles as being of superior authority in the Church by virtue of their proximity to the Lord. (See I Cor. 12:28 and Eph. 4:11.) But as Brunner has pointed out, this authority of apostolicity soon became a mechanical rather than an experiential matter,[11] a possibility which always exists.

The matter of authority is, of course, never an easy one with which to deal, and it can only be touched upon here. If we are true to our Protestant heritage, we must say that final authority lies only with God but that the nature of his will is mediated to us in various ways. The supreme authority is Jesus Christ, God's personal Word to us. Yet our knowledge of Jesus Christ, along with our knowledge of God's other self-revealing activity, is found in the record of God's revelation in the Bible. Thus in a real sense, though symbolically, not literally, the Bible is the basis of authority. Yet we cannot ignore, as some Protestants seek to do, either the activity of the Holy Spirit throughout the centuries of Christian history or the work of the Spirit in our midst today.[12] In greater or lesser degree, Protestant groups also recognize that the matter of reception of revelation is an individual matter, and thus no priest or minister can finally determine my reception of God's self-disclosure.

The question remains, then: what place does the special priesthood have in matters of faith and practice for the lay Christian? What

41

authority does the training and vocation of the ordained ministry bring with it? On a practical level, are all decisions on a local level to be made "democratically"? What are the means of seeking both the judgment of men and the leadership of the Spirit in the higher councils of the Church?

Without attempting a complete answer to this cluster of questions, three assertions may be made. For one thing, the person set aside to proclaim the gospel ought never to be prevented from so doing unless he clearly misinterprets the gospel. There is need for the prophet, for the voice crying in the wilderness, for the Amos and the John. Second, generally speaking, the carrying out of the work of the local church as well as of higher echelons ought to be done with the widest possible participation by both clergymen and the laity. Third, the minister-teacher-counselor will not hesitate to speak his convictions but he will not attempt to manipulate others into his convictions. In the final analysis the individual must be left free to make his own decision, and further he must assume a responsibility for his neighbor.

The Ministry of the Laity

It is significant that laymen have often been aware of their mission and have been dissatisfied with the manner in which the institutional church has allowed them to express it. In the first few centuries of the Church as it became more infected with the ways of the world, the monastic movement arose as a means whereby both the ordained and unordained might express in a more serious manner their sense of Christian vocation. The Protestant Reformation was in some ways a lay thrust, though its primary leadership did not always give the laity as significant a place in the life of the Church as was desired. The sectarian movement, represented by such groups as the Quakers, was again an expression of the understanding that the Church was composed of *all* the People of God. John Wesley gave greater place to the laity, especially through the use of lay preachers, though he was unwilling to put in practice all the implications of some of his ideas.

Within modern times, three significant movements have grown out of the desire of the unordained to have a more significant way of expressing their ministry in the Church. The first of these, the demand for lay participation in church government, is doubtless only partially a genuine expression of this concern, and surely represents partly the influence of democratic government upon church organization. It cannot be completely ignored from the former perspective, however.[13]

The second manifestation of this lay thrust in the nineteenth century consists of the various lay movements, most of them at first unofficial but later becoming official. The earliest of these was the Sunday-school movement, which had its inception in Gloucester, England, in 1780.[14] It was at first exclusively a lay movement, and was only gradually approved by and later adopted by the churches. By the 1830's, it had, to a great extent, been taken into the churches, but even after this it continued to be largely a lay-controlled and lay-operated movement. It was not until the second and third decades of the present century that it began to come under the domination of *professionally* employed workers on the national scale. Somewhat later local churches began to employ paid workers in Christian education. To a great extent the church-school movement remains a lay movement on the local level, though during recent decades this has become less and less the case at higher levels.

Another of these movements, that which dealt with college students, also had its beginning in the late eighteenth century, but did not become a movement of much importance until the late nineteenth.[15] The Student Christian Movement, with its various cognate groups, was largely lay centered, the great twentieth-century leader, John R. Mott, remaining a layman throughout his life. A correlative movement, youth work in the local church, was only partly a lay thrust, since much of the early leadership was ministerial. The various youth groups have in many ways been authentic lay movements, however.[16]

The women's groups, which began on the local church level prior to 1860 but began to be organized nationally after 1860, provide a further example of this lay thrust. These groups have on the whole remained under the complete control of laywomen.[17] The final of these movements is that concerned only with men. Such groups have never flourished like the others except for a time in the Brotherhood Movement of the early twentieth century.[18] In a real sense, however, the modern lay movement, to be discussed later, is a continuation of these men's groups.

A third manifestation of lay concern occurs in the modern "lay movement," currently one of the "signs of hope" in the Church. This was considered of enough importance that one of the studies made in preparation for the First Assembly of the World Council of Churches in 1948 concerned "The Training of Laymen in the Church." This memorandum first pointed to the renewed concern both for and by laymen, and then went on to ask whether this simply indicates an interest in "using the latent forces of its members for the effective execution of its service to the world, and for the customary work of the Church." In other words, is there simply a concern that laymen be *used* by the Church in carrying out its multitudinous tasks? There is this, the pamphlet continues, but it would also appear that there is "A deeper and wider concern . . . a radical reorientation of the Church as a whole, as to its function and service to the world, and as to its conception of what a layman is."

This, then, necessitates

a clear theology about the place which the layman, the ordinary church member, has in the Church, in all seriousness taken as the *Body* of Christ, the new community that the Holy Spirit calls to life when the message of God's redemption of the world in Christ is proclaimed, not as a message floating above the world scene, but as one entering into, struggling with it, and changing it.

Thus, the membership of the Church, the clergy included, "is primarily 'laikos' (from which the word 'lay' derives), because the Church is the 'laos,' the people of God. Never in the history of the Church have the consequences of this simple but central fact of the New Testament message been fully thought out, nor adequately transformed into a practice in the life of congregations and churches."

Were this change to take place in the thinking of the Church, then

a real and fundamental change in the life of the churches will take place. Then the Church will not announce its message and do its deeds in complex modern life as a mere agency which uses to the best of its ability its voluntary army of workers—which is, fundamentally speaking, a secular act, and not a Christian one—but as a body of people, who live, witness, and work in the world because of their divine vocation.[19]

It will be noted that those who prepared this study memorandum recognized the profound difference between simply *using* laymen to do the work of the Church and the revolutionary fact of laymen's *being* the Church, the *Body* of Christ. This point of view is the one implied in the previous chapter of this present study, and it is the one which will be further explored in succeeding chapters.

Nor was the Second Assembly of the World Council of Churches any less concerned with this matter of implementing the concept of the priesthood of believers. One of the six subtopics for the Assembly was "The Laity—the Christian in His Vocation." In the introduction to the official document provided for this section, this statement occurs:

In many churches all over the world in recent years some fresh movement has arisen, not organized from above but born of a widely and deeply felt need on the part of the Church to meet man in the modern world where he really lives and of a new joyousness on the part of its members in witnessing to Jesus Christ as Saviour and Lord of all realms of life. It is through its lay membership that the Church enters into real and daily contact with the workaday world and shares in its problems and aspirations. It is in the life and work of the lay membership that the Church must manifest in the world its regenerative and redemptive power. One of the greatest tasks of the Church today is to grasp clearly the significance of the lay ministry *in* the world.[20]

Manifestations of this interest are not confined to discussion alone. Especially in Europe have various lay movements arisen, the most famous of these being the Iona Community off the coast of Scotland. In Germany, in particular, since World War II professional and other lay groups have emerged. The Ecumenical Institute held in connection with the World Council of Churches in Boissey, Switzerland, is another example. Such centers in the United States as Brighton, Michigan, and Pendle Hill are illustrative of the new lay thrust. These and similar expressions will be considered at greater length in a subsequent chapter.[21]

All of this points to the need for a continual discussion of the meaning of the Church and the place of laymen in the fellowship. It further indicates that any theory or practical strategy for the Church which becomes clerically or professionally dominated is likely to be resisted by laymen. Whether this is done through an understanding of the nature of the Church or whether other motives enter in, we may be thankful that God is able to work through ordinary church members to call its professional leaders back to a reconsideration of the true nature of the Church.

The People of God

One of the central concepts in our thinking about the Church, then, must be the idea of the people of God, those whom God has called to special mission among his other human children. The crux of the matter is whether those who have responded to the call of God in Christ take seriously this call. The people of God—*laos,* ordained and unordained, professional and voluntary—are mutually responsible to God and to one another. This call is expressed in various forms of service—through worship of God, through mutual edification, through pastoral oversight, through service to fellow churchmen and to those outside the church, through action within society. This is the theological basis for our lay program of teaching, evangelism, and outreach. It is the motivation which sends the Church through individuals throughout the world to proclaim and teach the gospel. In the Christian community, there can be no such thing as placing this responsibility upon a few. The few are set aside to perform special functions, but the work of the Church, in its interior life and in its outreach into the world, is the responsibility of all those who are the people of God.

In a time when specialization and professionalism are among the prevailing characteristics of our Western culture, it is not easy for the Church to take seriously its peculiar quality as an elected people. It is tempting to go along with these cultural trends and thus allow the Church to become primarily an institution presided over by professionals, including the ordained clergy. To do so, however, is a denial of the very nature of the Christian community. Thus it is imperative that the Church stand against these cultural trends and proclaim its message that

in Christ Jesus you are all sons of God, through faith. For as many of you as were baptized into Christ have put on Christ. There is neither Jew nor Greek, there is neither slave nor free, there is neither male nor female; for you are all one in Christ Jesus. (Gal. 3:26-28.)

IV

The Fellowship of the Spirit

"Where two or three are gathered in my name, there am I in the midst of them."

(Matt. 18:20.)

WHAT HAS BEEN SAID THUS FAR ABOUT THE CHURCH IS, IN A SENSE, prologue to the key concept concerning its nature as a redemptive fellowship. Because of many misunderstandings concerning the meaning of fellowship, however, it is essential that we see the Church first as an expression of the life of God in the world and second as the response of men to the call of God. Then, and only then, can we begin to understand the meaning of the Church as a redemptive fellowship.

Before proceeding to our discussion of the nature of fellowship, then, it is appropriate that we remind ourselves again that the Church is the Body of Christ, a social organism into which individuals are born first by water through baptism, later by the Spirit through personal response to the activity of the Spirit. They are engrafted into Christ's Body. This body of believers is called to be the People of God, the new Israel, a royal priesthood in which there is neither bond nor free, Jew nor Greek, ordained nor unordained, since all are one in Christ Jesus. The people of God are mutually responsible before God, one for the other, and for witnessing to their faith in the larger community outside the Church.

In describing the nature of the Church, however, no single concept is more fundamental than that of its reality as the redemptive fellowship. This is true when one considers both its nature and its mission. Its mission is expressed through various ministries, or functions, as we shall see in subsequent chapters. Prior to any of its functions, however, is *what it is.* Unless it is truly a redemptive fellowship in its relationships, both to its own constituency and to the world beyond, it cannot speak effectively a *word* of salvation. Prior to what the Church *does* or *says* is what it *is*.[1] Just as the individual speaks first through who he is, then by what he says, so does the Church. Unless the Church, in its local as well as its larger manifestations, is in some real sense a community which bears the character of fellowship, its voice of redemption will not be heard.

Mistaken Notions of "Fellowship"

One wishes at the outset that there were a better word than "fellowship" to use in describing this aspect of the life of the Church. As we shall see later, such words as "partnership," "communion," and "participation" may be used as synonyms for the Greek word *koinonia*, though none of these is quite satisfactory. The very fact that the word "fellowship" is so widely used, however, behooves us to come to a deeper understanding of what the term signifies.

Indeed no word is used more glibly in the speech of the Church than "fellowship," so much so that some church members, with reason, have reacted against its use at all. It has recently become the official designation of all youth groups participating in the United Christian Youth Movement, and thus we have the Westminster Fellowship, the Christian Youth Fellowship, the Methodist Youth Fellowship. Further, one of the five program areas of the Youth Fellowship is called Christian Fellowship. In fact, any analysis of the program of the local church usually includes a discussion on fellowship. Certainly there is no end to the emphasis upon fellowship in the modern church.

But the question must be asked: How much of this is really *Christian* fellowship and how much is simply conviviality, what may be designated, without any disrespect to luncheon clubs, as "Rotary Club fellowship"? Far too often that which goes under the name of fellowship in the Church is not essentially different from that which characterizes nonchurch groups.

Several mistakes are current in our thinking concerning the nature of Church fellowship. For one thing, there is a general impression that it can be produced as, let us say, one builds a table. Devices, techniques, "tricks of the trade," are employed in order to bring about fellowship. To be sure there are means of encouraging fellowship, and a subsequent chapter will consider some of these ways. Yet there can be no assurance that any of these devices will lead to anything deeper than conviviality. Christian fellowship is something that happens

48

as a result of the operation of the Spirit, and human contrivances may be a hindrance as well as a help in setting the conditions under which the Spirit can become known.

Related to this mistake is a similar one: namely, that fellowship is a distinct and separate phase of the work of the Church. Perhaps it is necessary functionally to have a committee, commission, or program area set up to be concerned with fellowship, but to think of this group as being solely responsible for, or capable of, making the Church into a fellowship is a great mistake. It is significant that those who set up the present youth program through the United Christian Youth Movement have sought to avoid this, since there is a "program area," not a commission, responsible for seeking means of bringing about fellowship throughout the youth program. It is quite possible that the deepest sense of fellowship will emerge out of a project which a group carries out, even though it may involve manual work. As a mater of fact, the work camps which have become a part of the youth program are one of the significant examples of Christian fellowship.

A third mistake common to our thinking is that fellowship in the Church is on a human level only, and further that the fellowship of the Spirit is an individual fellowship, while fellowship with one another is social. We often forget the statement attributed to Jesus, "Where two or three are gathered in my name, there am I in the midst of them" (Matt. 18:20). Since this is so near to the heart of the meaning of Christian *koinonia*, this will be discussed at greater length in subsequent pages.

A fourth mistake is the opposite of what has just been stated: whereas Christian fellowship is more than conviviality and while discussion in distinctly religious terms will normally be a part of Christian fellowship, pious words and phrases do not create fellowship. Some of the bitterest feelings arise in the midst of theological discussions! In some circles the two subjects most under taboo are politics and religion. This is illustrated by a statement made by a theological professor a few years ago concerning the difference in atmosphere of a church meeting and a so-called "secular" group which he had attended successively. The first, a meeting of leaders in the field of Christian education, so he felt, was accompanied by almost bitter feelings and a lack of acceptance by the various members of each other in their differences. The latter, a meeting concerned with better human relationships, on the other hand, was characterized by complete acceptance

49

of the varying members even though there were wide differences in thinking among the members of the group.

Further, even when there is reasonable agreement and almost a unanimity of opinion in a Church group, mere pious cant can never be thought of as a substitute for the working of the Spirit through a human group.

All of this adds up to the conclusion that fellowship on a Christian level is something which, like man's salvation, is given to him, yet something which does not become operative until man meets certain conditions. It is significant that Jesus said, "Where two or three are gathered *in my name,* there am I in the midst of them." It should be obvious that being gathered *in the name of* Jesus means being together in his Spirit.

The Meaning of Koinonia

What, then, is the meaning of the "Fellowship of the Spirit"?

As we have said, we are dealing here with the very heart of the Church itself. There is wide disagreement over many questions concerning the nature of the Church, its ministry, and its sacraments. One need only read recent volumes produced under the auspices of the World Council of Churches to have this brought to mind most vividly. There is an increasing awareness, however, that near the heart of the meaning of the Church is the concept of *koinonia.* Brunner has put it this way: "The togetherness of Christian men is thus not secondary or contingent: it is integral to their life just as is their abiding in Christ." [2] And in conclusion he asserts, "Here lies the essence of the New Testament *Ecclesia*—the oneness of communion with Christ by faith and brotherhood in love." [3]

J. Robert Nelson, in his analysis of the doctrines of the church, writes even more emphatically concerning the centrality of the concept of *koinonia.* His witness is a telling one because of his wide study of the divergences among the beliefs of theologians concerning the nature of the Church. The following extensive quotation is his summary of the matter:

When all has been said about the Body of Christ—its meaning in the New Testament, its relationship to Christ as the Head, and its organic nature—we emerge from the tangles of theological discussion and argumentation, still somewhat confused and a little weary, and witness in the plain light of experience that rare quality which makes the Church truly the Body of Christ: the *koinōnia*. Just as the first Christians, when they became members of the Body, found that they had become bound to one another by common ties, which were even stronger than those natural ties of family, race, religion and nation, so this *koinōnia* has characterized the communal life of the Church in every generation of its history, varying in degree, to be sure, but never lacking altogether. We have already considered at length in Chapter Two how the *koinōnia* is regarded as a work of the Holy Spirit, as participation of persons in the gifts of God. The concept of the Body of Christ does not alter this meaning, but supplements and enlarges it for our understanding.[4]

In a sense all of this has already been said in the analysis of the Church as the Body of Christ and as the People of God. In order to make the picture clearer, however, a discussion of the meaning of *koinonia* seems necessary.

Actually in human associations generally this quality of *koinonia* may be partially realized, though not all common associations reach this level. Much of life is lived on a surface level, especially in a culture which often throws people together (as on a subway train or a crowded elevator) but often provides for them nothing to hold in common. Unfortunately, even in human association where this deeper level ought to be realized it often is not. This is even true within family groups where there is so little shared in common that the members of the family hardly know each other in a significant fashion. Any analysis of juvenile delinquency is likely to reveal that one factor which entered into its cause is the failure of parents to provide the love and acceptance needed by teen-agers.

Why is this the case? Is it not partly the fact that common loyalties, common enterprises, the necessity to function as a family group, have tended to break down? Some time ago I visited on a ranch in New Mexico, ten miles from the nearest post office, thirty miles from the nearest telephone, several miles from the nearest neighbor. In such a situation family solidarity is natural. Although this is an exaggeration of the situation which prevailed in the United States prior to our highly mechanized and technological culture, our former culture did provide more natural ties which bound the family into a fellowship. There was more reason why a family group *had* to function as a family. Today if a family is to develop "togetherness," there must be a deliberate effort to plan opportunities for developing it.[5] The slogan, "The family that prays together stays together," may reflect an inadequate theology of prayer, but it represents a realistic portrayal of the family situation.

What has been said concerning the family is true of other human groupings also. For example, men in the armed forces often develop a deep sense of camaraderie which at least partakes of real fellowship This may be based on loyalty to the "outfit," in the sharing of hardships and danger, in the sheer necessity of obtaining from one another the satisfactions necessary for human living. One of the things that makes war bearable is this fellowship which emerges. This same thing may happen in various groups and clubs in civilian life. In fact, wherever there is a deep sense of participation in something which binds the group together, mutuality is likely to develop. However, unless a grouping of people has something other than mere contiguity to bind them *together,* they are not likely to become anything other than an association of people.[6]

It is essentially this factor of participation that is often neglected in our discussion of Christian fellowship; yet the meaning of the word *koinonia,* the New Testament word sometimes translated as "fellowship," always involves this. Studies that have been made of the word *koinonia* and its cognates all agree that the meaning is more than association. Campbell, in perhaps the most complete analysis of the words *koinonos, koinon (eiv),* and *koinonia,* points out that these words all come from the root *koin* which means "one who has *something* in common with *someone* else." [7] Thus *koinonia,* which is sometimes translated "fellowship," sometimes as "partnership," sometimes as "communion," refers to "the having of *something* in common with *someone.*" [8]

L. S. Thornton, who has also made an extensive study of the concept, emerges with an identical conclusion. Quoting from M. R. Vincent in the *International Critical Commentary* on Phil. 1:5, he writes: "Now *koinonia* 'involves common and mutual interest and participation in a common object.' The word means 'partnership' or 'sharing' of persons in something." [9] He writes further: *"[Koinonia]* is not simply a new form of human fellowship. Its distinctive character is wholly derived from the fact that it is a fellowship, not only of man with man, but also of man with God." [10] Later he adds: "The life which we share in common in the Church is not primarily that of a human fellowship. Its distinctive character as manifested in human fellowship is wholly drawn from a divine source, and mediated to us in that fellowship through our joint-participation in Christ." [11]

Nelson agrees with this definition as the following passage indicates:

Most scholars are agreed that the fundamental idea which *koinōnia* conveys is that of "participation in something in which others participate."

This definition is sharply distinguished from the generally held, but inaccurate, notion that the word means simply "fellowship," in the sense of association with other persons. Other English words which come close to being adequate renderings of the Greek, in its primary meaning, are "sharing," "joint possession," and "holding in common."

But in New Testament usage there is nearly always the connotation of participation in something *with* someone else.[14]

The inescapable conclusion, then, is that the New Testament concept of *koinonia* implies more than mere human association. It involves participation in something which is held in common, that common reality being the Spirit that was in Christ Jesus and that is still available through the Holy Spirit. No view of church fellowship which conceives of it as common association alone is true to the New Testament view.

Participation in the Spirit

As one seeks to delineate the meaning of *koinonia*, he is made aware anew of the two sides of the Church which were presented in a previous chapter.[15] The Church is God's gift through Christ—it is his Body—but the Church is also those who have entered into a personal covenant with God through Christ and have thus become his people. Paul expresses this dual nature in words written to the Philippians:

So if there is any encouragement in Christ, any incentive of love, and participation [*koinonia*] in the Spirit, any affection and sympathy, complete my joy by being of the same mind, having the same love, being in full accord and of one mind. (Phil. 2:1-2.)

J. B. Phillips' translation of this passage makes clear the two sides of the equation, the first part being a conditional clause, the second being a command based on the conditions stated:

Now if your experience of Christ's encouragement and love means anything to you, if you have known something of the fellowship of His Spirit, and all that it means in kindness and deep sympathy, do make my best hopes for you come true! Live together in harmony, live together in love, as though you had only one mind and one spirit between you.[16]

To state it more positively, when we have participated in ("had fellowship with") the Spirit of Christ, then the result is that we can live in harmony and love, "as though you had only one mind and one spirit between you." God's action precedes man's response, which is the basic formula for Christian ethics.

Although we must confess that we are dealing here with a mystery which defies complete human analysis, it is not enough that we leave the issue here. It is necessary, then, that we recognize that the Church comes to us out of the past as a gift, a gift which had its inception in Jesus of Nazareth whom Christians, through the eyes of faith, call Son of God and Son of man. The existence of the Church comes to us as an objective fact with a history and a tradition, grounded in the Biblical witness to the original events which called it into being. When we strip away the human accretions, this is what we find beneath these human contrivings.

Again it may be appropriate to use the family as an illustration. We are born into a family with a tradition, with customs and habitual ways of doing things, with standards and values. Whether these are adequate or inadequate, they come to us as a gift. If they are the former, then they come as a gracious gift to us and provide for us the beginning of a full and rich life. As a child, we participate in what is given, for better or worse, however, and we can never completely disassociate ourselves from what we are as a result of our family background. We may reject our family and seek to start out again, but we can never fully do so. If we accept it, then we enter into its spirit and become a participating member of the family fellowship, a fact which lasts beyond any geographical relationship to our particular family. Our family has entered into us and we in turn have entered into it.

So it is with the Church. We enter into what exists, what has been given to us. Any particular local church may or may not give to us the true Spirit of Christ, but even when it has repudiated its heritage in part the residue is there. If there is any remnant of the *true* Church, this comes to us as well as the human accretions which have overlaid the true Church. Part of our personal response may be *reform*, but it is reform, not a complete beginning again. This is why the Bible, as the primary witness to God's activity, has served and must continue to serve, as a means whereby the renewal of the Church may take place.

It is this matter of *personal response* which provides the other side of our understanding of the Church. Revelation of God comes through the Church, but we must respond individually. Thus, while the *koinonia* is a gift to us, it is also of our doing in the sense that our personal response makes it possible for God to create among us the *koinonia*. The response of the individual Christian must be to God, not to the institutional church. But the ordinary means by which his response is evoked is through the community of the Church, however inadequate that community may now be. In this process of renewal, there must be a continual calling to mind of the original revelation which created the Church, God making himself known through Jesus Christ, as recorded in the New Testament.

The ways in which God's gift comes to us, then, consist both of the Church as it now exists and the Church as it was meant to be, as the original revelation in the New Testament describes it. We cannot disassociate ourselves from the gift that comes to us through the existing Church, just as the reformers did not. We can seek to be an instrument of renewal as we enter into the original meaning of the Church through the Scriptures and respond to the Spirit revealed there. It is never enough that we simply take; we must also give. And the giving involves our responding to the God revealed in Jesus Christ and witnessed to by the Biblical record. This personal response will be discussed in the following chapter in more detail.

The truth is, as we well know, that the Church is often more of a social club than it is the Fellowship of the Spirit. When this happens, fellowship invariably descends to the level of conviviality, and the motivation for evangelism becomes community betterment rather than new life in Christ. On the other hand, we may easily confuse pious words and phrases with the Spirit of Christ. In neither case has participation in the Spirit of Christ resulted. Through our personal response to the Spirit, the Spirit may be freed to act among us to effect the unity which involves "being of the same mind, having the same love, being in full accord and of one mind." This mind is nothing short of the mind of Christ.

Koinonia *and the Living Church*

As we face up to the failure of the Church to be a redemptive fellowship, we are reminded that a practical as well as a theological consideration is involved here. That is, nothing short of the Spirit of God in Christ is likely to transcend the natural barriers which divide men into classes, races, social groups, and the like. Most churches tend to be race and class churches, which is the *natural* thing. All persons *do* tend to seek those of their own status in life, with their interests and concerns. So long as our churches remain cultural institutions, it is doubtful if anything else is possible. Further, so long as "fellowship" activities are thought of primarily as recreation and social life (which do have a place in the life of the local church), not much is likely to be done to bridge the race and class biases which divide us.

To recognize this as the *natural* tendency is not to approve it, however. Rather we ought to bow in repentance at our failure to allow the Spirit of Christ to be among us. Although the early Church consisted largely of those of the lower strata of society, it was not exclusively so. And thus Paul could write to Philemon, the master, concerning Onesimus, the slave, that Philemon was to receive him "no longer as a slave but more than a slave, as a beloved brother" (Philem. 16). Whatever divisions existed were overcome whenever the Spirit was active in a local situation, as is illustrated by the story of Pentecost (Acts 2) and the nature of the early community as described in Acts 2:44-47 and 4:32-34.[17] (See also Gal. 3:28.) This is not to imply that there were never divisions. The conflict between Peter and Paul, and the divisions in the Church at Corinth, did exist. The remarkable thing is not that such divisions came about but rather that so great a degree of unity could be achieved in spite of them.

As we view the Church today, we cannot help being struck by its inadequacies as a redemptive fellowship. We are divided into denominations, and denominations are divided into race and class churches. Individual local churches often are torn by inner strife. There is bickering and strife over petty matters. Much of our activity is pointless and thus reflects the poverty of our inner life. The superficiality of much of our church life reveals the inadequacy of our faith.

This failure of the Church to be a redemptive fellowship poses for us the problem of a starting point for its transformation and renewal. If God must work through us, where do we begin? It is much the same problem that must be faced on the personal level when we confront the need for psychic healing. Day-by-day therapy leading to healthy selfhood takes place in the experience of acceptance in the family and other groups. Emotionally disturbed children especially need such love.

Yet how can parents really accept their children and provide for them an atmosphere which develops healthy selfhood when they themselves have so seldom known the feeling of being accepted for what they are? How can even the therapist, be he professional or pastoral, know sufficiently this experience of acceptance unless he has himself undergone therapy?

In other words, if a healing relationship is necessary to begin psychological healing, who is able to provide it? This is a vicious circle, as anyone familiar with the case material concerning problem children knows. The truth of the matter is, however, that we must begin where we are in this process. We begin with whatever love, acceptance, and understanding we are capable of giving and trust in the working of the Spirit to bring about the healing which is needed. Our love is imperfect, but, as Reuel Howe has said, we trust that God can use our love as a means by which someone can become receptive to the love of God.[18]

So it is in every local church fellowship. It may be that a local church, even as an individual, may become so hardened, so insensitive to human need, so sealed off from the Spirit of God, that it has cut itself off from hope. But certainly this is the rare exception, if it exists at all. In most, if not all, congregations, there is enough love, acceptance, and forgiveness for a start to be made. There is enough sensitivity to the Holy Spirit that God can act. And though this is a vicious circle— namely, that the person in deep need must have the acceptance of others, yet they may not have known it sufficiently to give it—it is also an expanding circle. For the giving of love brings back love in return. The sharing of one's inadequate faith lends faith in turn. The acceptance, even partially, of another person makes it possible for him to begin to accept himself and others.

Thus, the recognition by a few in a congregation of the importance of the Church's *being* a redemptive fellowship may be the beginning of transformation. Through them the Spirit may be able to work for renewal. It was only two or three in whose midst Jesus promised to be. It was a motley crew to whom the Spirit came at Pentecost. It was in the little Holy Club that the Wesleyan revival which stirred England and reached to America originated.

The beginning of such a transformation is in relationships, as we have repeatedly implied. Yet this is not to discredit the importance of a clear note of forgiveness being spoken from pulpit and lectern. Many may need a note of judgment before they are ready either to be forgiven or to forgive; others are already aware of judgment and cry for a voice of mercy. Even when judgment is proclaimed, it must be followed by a clear statement of the grace, mercy, and forgiveness of God.

If Tillich and May[19] and countless others are right in affirming that our age is one of anxiety, particularly the anxiety of emptiness and meaninglessness, then the place where *koinonia* comes into being may be as we seek to deal with the everyday threats to human existence and its meaning. It may be that we must begin by dealing with the boredom associated with much modern labor, the gnawing sense of the futility of acquiring many possessions, the threat to existence in modern atomic war, the loss of nerve occasioned by wars and rumors of war, the emptiness with which many people face the endless round of duties of the day, the deep anguish which comes from the destruction by science of our illusions about our own importance in the universe, the loss of any structure in which life can find meaning. At these points persons may respond to the fellowship which is offered to them, however inadequate it may be. As God is able to work through this human fellowship, then perhaps they can know themselves loved and accepted by God. As this process goes on then the renewal of the Church is also taking place.

In other words, by deed and by word we who preach and teach must make known the reality and the power of God's love, acceptance, and forgiveness. Although this is known more easily through relationships, it also is known through words. Modern man, with his deep anxiety, his need to belong, his loss of moorings, needs, more than he realizes, the *koinonia* of the Christian community. We cannot *build* the fellowship: it is, in the final analysis, God's gift. We can respond to God's gift and be a means through which it may be offered to others as we relate to our fellow men in understanding and acceptance of the deep longings of the human self.

The beginnings may seem inadequate, but God can use even feeble efforts to reveal his love. As this happens, the Church is present as a redeeming and sustaining fellowship. The Church is then acting as the Church, and its ministry—its "functioning"—has become consistent with its true nature.

V

The Call of God

"I therefore . . . beg you to lead a life worthy of the calling to which you have been called."

(*Eph. 4:1.*)

OUR CONCERN THUS FAR HAS BEEN FOCUSED PRINCIPALLY ON THE Church as a corporate body: the Body of Christ, the People of God, the redemptive fellowship. All of these point to the fact that the Church is an organism into which individuals are born, but concomitantly they also remind us that the Church either exists as a body of men joined to the living Lord or it does not exist at all. The figure used in John 15 is an apt one: "I am the vine, you are the branches. He who abides in me, and I in him, he it is that bears much fruit." Branches (individuals) must be attached to the vine, and are thus related to the head of the Church (Christ) as well as to one another. Yet each branch is unique. Each person must respond *in person* to the call of God and bear fruit in his life.

The dilemma which was faced in the previous chapter must be considered again: namely, that the Church must *be* a redemptive fellowship in order to draw persons into a redemptive relationship with Christ. On the other hand, the Church cannot be this kind of fellowship except as individuals have responded personally to the redemptive love of God. The Church, while coming to us as a gift, must also be accepted with a sense of obligation. The individual, when he has been spoken to redemptively, must then respond in terms of commitment and faith.

To put this another way, individuals to whom the Gospel has spoken meaningfully must take seriously the call which comes to them and become responsible participants in the covenant community. Whatever love and forgiveness they have known must be shared with others in order that they too may hear the call of God to responsible citizenship in his Kingdom. The Christian's vocation is to live responsibly before God and his fellow men.

The Meaning of Christian Vocation

The burden of this chapter, then, is that the Church must present to men the call of God in Christ and that individuals must respond to that call in terms of the totality of their existence. Men must take so seriously their Christian vocation that the dichotomy beween worship and work, sacred and secular, Sunday and weekday, is broken down. The only effective means through which the Christian witness can be made today is the laity, that is, all the people of God. All, including clergymen, must witness to their faith in their daily work, in their social life, in politics, and in every other area of life.

We shall use the term "Christian vocation" as that which most adequately describes what is meant here. To be sure, there are other words in the Christian's vocabulary which describe parts of this experience. "Dedication," "commitment," "conversion," "sanctification"—all are good words, but partial in their connotation. "Stewardship" is the nearest to being inclusive, but even it has been widely abused. Conversion too often is thought of as implying the change from one set of morals to another, and nothing else. Thus many people who are converted to a higher set of morals are not converted with respect to their business life, political life, and social life. Commitment and dedication have too often been associated with life apart from daily existence; they have been "spiritualized" to the point where they have little reference to the rough-and-tumble existence of market place, assembly line, office, and professional life. Stewardship is a good word, but has too frequently been used as a synonym for proportionate giving, and even when it is applied to time, ability, and other factors in life other than possessions, it is usually used as if one part of life belongs to God and the other to man.

There is an increasing tendency to go back into the Christian tradition for another of those largely forgotten concepts as the most adequate to describe what we mean when we speak of a response to God in terms of all of life. This term, "Christian vocation," must also be reinterpreted, of course, since it is commonly used to describe full-time church work. In its biblical and Reformation sense, however, it was given a much broader meaning, referring to the entire range of human doing. Therefore, the word "vocation" is chosen, since it points to the totality of our existence in a manner different from other traditional words.

The biblical basis for this concept of Christian vocation has been clearly stated in recent years.[1] Unlike Greek thought, which considered work as an unmitigated curse and leisure as the gift of the gods, the Bible evaluates daily work not only as honorable but also as part of God's call to man to be man. God calls each person into his service, and man's service partly involves his daily work. As Minear puts it, "There is one vocation (call) for all, yet each has his own distinctive work to do. Wherever present labor does not advance his vocation, that labor is sinful and futile." [2] Richardson writes in a like manner: "Our secular occupations are to be regarded not as ends in themselves but as means to the service of the Kingdom of God. They have Christian value only in so far as they can be made means to the end of the Gospel." [3] The Christian will not follow any and all occupations, but in that which he does follow he will serve with a joy and a freedom that makes of his work as well as his worship a service to God, and thus his work will also serve his fellow men.

Although this concept apparently was obscured rather early in the history of the Christian movement, it was preserved in many of the monastic orders. Calhoun has shown how close a relationship existed between work and worship in many of the orders. Manual labor was generally required, a condition which persisted for several centuries in most orders and even to the present in some. But outside the monastery the relation of faith and daily life tended to be lost, especially as the gap between the monastery and daily life widened.

The ordering of life which had been gradually developing was wrought into a system by the thirteenth-century theologian Thomas Aquinas, who sought to bring all of life into one hierarchical plan. Although his hierarchy included manual workers as well as others, and though it may be said that all occupations are considered honorable by Aquinas, nevertheless "spiritual" works are put at the top of the hierarchy and manual work at the bottom.[4] Thus, in the Roman Catholic system those who carry on the work of the Church are considered to be on a more exalted plain than those who do, let us say, manual work. And though this theoretically is not the Protestant position, most Protestants tend to maintain his same dichotomy between the various occupations.

The Reformers discovered again the meaning of Christian vocation, a fact which makes it difficult to reconcile the later double standard (between "personal" and "social" life, between the sacred and the secular) which developed in Lutheranism. Calhoun has summarized Luther's thought as follows:

> There are diversities of gifts, of responsibilities, and of service, some very small, some very great in range and complexity. But whether one be a simple householder, a magistrate, or a prince of the realm, each believer can know his status in the perspective of the Christian faith as, equally with every other, a calling appointed by God. There is no such thing as a profane or merely secular order from which God is absent, and in which God is not to be served.[5]

That this concept, held also to some extent by Calvin, did not prevail is obvious as one recalls the development of Protestant thought in the years following. As a new economic order was forged out, the concept of responsibility before God within all areas of life was more and more lost. The term "vocation" gradually came to mean one's occupation, secular if carried on outside the Church, sacred if done within the Church. The call of God was gradually transformed into the narrower conception of the "call to preach," [6] and the broader interpretation of Christian vocation was largely obscured.

How *far* this trend developed is illustrated by the resistance which developed in the late nineteenth and early twentieth centuries to the attempts made by followers of the "social gospel" to reassert the relevance of the gospel to social and economic life.[7] Within recent years we have experienced another effort on the part of the extreme right wing to silence those who would indicate the relevance of the gospel to all areas of life. And in one sense these laymen are right: on the whole, ministers do not know enough about business and economic life to speak with any authority in such matters. They ought not to feel compelled to speak on such issues, for that matter. So long, however, as laymen fail to take seriously the implications of their faith in business and political life, sensitive ordained ministers will no doubt feel under compulsion to remind those in these areas of their responsibilities as Christians. To be sure, such exhortations will not usually change economic and social practices, but it is possible that they *will* awaken those in positions of responsibility to discharge their duties in the light of the Christian faith. Actually, however, it is only when those involved themselves relate their faith to all areas of life that anything will happen.

The Rediscovery of "Christian Vocation"

In our day we are witnessing a rediscovery of the meaning of Christian vocation in its biblical and Reformation sense. Although for many people the term still implies an occupation carried out in the name of the Church, its larger meaning is increasingly known and employed. It is in this sense that W. R. Forrester uses the word in the title of his important contribution to our thinking, the Cunningham Lectures at New College, Edinburgh, delivered in 1950: *Christian Vocation: Studies in Faith and Work*.[8] A similar title, "The Laity— The Christian in His Vocation," was used as the subject of one of the study groups for the World Council of Churches' meeting in 1954.[9] Others have preferred to emphasize the same concept in the phrase, "the Christian in his daily work," or some similar one. For example, one of the most recent contributions to this area of thought is called *Work and Vocation: A Christian Discussion*.[10]

Whatever terms are used, two primary factors are involved in them. First, there is a recognition that God calls a person to his service in the totality of everyday existence, with the consequent breakdown of the division of sacred and secular callings. Second, there is a realization that the Church can be effective in our complex civilization only as those *not* engaged in its professional activities witness to Christ in the world in which they live. In those areas of the world where the ministry of the Church is either ignored or ridiculed, this would seem of particular significance.

The document prepared for the Second Assembly of the World Council of Churches on the laity has already been cited.[11] In it there is a recognition not only of the theological soundness of a view which involves each Christian in a personal response of witnessing to his faith; there is also the frank admission that only in such a lay witness can the Church enter into and thus be a medium for the transformation of both the lives of individuals and of the life of society. "It is through its lay membership that the Church enters into real and daily contact with the workaday world and shares in its problems and aspirations. It is in the life and work of the lay membership that the Church must manifest in the world its regenerative and redemptive power." [12]

Further, when there is such a recognition of the universality of God's call to responsible service from *all* those who accept his grace,

The trained theologian, the pastor and missionary, instead of being regarded as *the* evangelist of the Church—a job for which he is in a particularly bad position—will then be the biblical and theological instructor of the evangelists, a job for which he is in a particularly good position. The Church as a whole will not speak too frequently in much debated pronouncements; it will speak no less officially but in a less static and more dynamic way by the decisions Christians make daily in their life in society.[13]

It should be clearly noted that the reason for a renewed emphasis on God's call to every man is *not* to promote the institution of the Church. We are not primarily concerned with new techniques of evangelism or with ways of "building up your church"—though it should be added that we are much concerned with evangelism as such and with the well-being of the local congregation and the Church generally.

If this concept of Christian vocation is taken seriously, indeed, it may well be that the local church as such will demand *less* time from many laymen who are now serving on committees and are doing other work generally designated as "church work." This will be the case in order that these laymen can devote more time and energy to the wider calling of which we are speaking. Too much of the concern of the modern church, as has already been noted, is that laymen be *used* by the church to promote its interest. What we are saying here is that laymen *are* the Church and that they are doing "Church work" as they live and witness as Christians in their everyday work. "Church work is the service a Christian gives for Christ in his everyday work and play and home life. Church work that counts is simply living for Christ every day right where we are." [14]

The Church and the Call of God

The implications of this concept of Christian vocation concern both the nature and the mission of the Church. One of the problems which we have repeatedly faced as we sought to describe the Church in corporate terms has been the necessity also of finding a way of speaking of individual response. The life of the Church—the revelation from God which comes to men through the Church—must be internalized; it must find individual expression. Life is social in nature, but each individual must be *himself* as well as a part of various groups. So the Church is a corporate Body, but it is also a community of believers who take seriously their call from God. *Koinonia* is a gift from God, but, as the previous chapter insisted, individual response to the gift is the primary manner in which the gift is made available to others.

It is at this point that the dual nature of the Church becomes most obvious. The *ekklēsia* is the People of God called into his service, but this call must be internalized and responded to individually. The call of God to every man to live responsibly before him is the Christian's vocation. The corporate Body cannot finally tell each individual *how* he must respond to God: it does—and must—call him to this personal response. It is through the Church, with its written Book, the Bible, that this call is made clear to the individual believer, but his particular response is his own.

If the Church's *nature* cannot be understood fully apart from some understanding of how the individual responds, it is even clearer that the *mission* of the Church cannot be described without reference to this personal response. Indeed, its mission is likely to be thought of primarily in institutional terms unless the concept of Christian vocation such as has already been described is kept in mind. When the Church is considered as primarily an institution, then those responsible for the ongoing life of the church—ordained and professional leaders, as well as "leading laymen"—may be interested in "using the latent forces of the laity," but they are not likely to think of the Church as expressing itself primarily *through* the laity. On the other hand, when we see clearly that the meaning of God's call to everyman involves a total response from him, we shall no longer think primarily of what the layman can contribute to the life of the institutional church (though this is involved); rather we shall think first of how the layman—everyman—can live as a Christian in the totality of his existence.

To be sure, the ongoing enterprise of the local, regional, and national church must have the devoted service of both the professional leader and the nonprofessional (unpaid) worker. Clergymen; professional, ordained or unordained workers such as Directors of Christian Education, executive secretaries, various types of administrators, and the like; and laymen (used here to designate those not in paid positions)—all are necessary for the institutional life of the Church. To deny the necessity of such life, as Niebuhr has reminded us, is unrealistic.[15]

Administration, as we shall later see, is the Church in action. In our complex culture the institutional church shares in the growing complexities of all of the institutions of our society, and free, voluntary service to the institutional church is both necessary and valid.

But if we are careful to preserve the biblical concept of God's call to man, we shall see that the work of the Church—which is fundamentally the work of Christ—is not done *only* through the local, regional, or national institution. At times, indeed, these organizations may actually get in the way of the work of Christ by demanding too much of the time of its constituency. God's work must also be done *in the world*. The Church is not just an institution of human betterment, as we have tried to make clear. It is not a secret society whose conditions for membership are fulfilled through loyalty to the institution. Rather, it is the Body of Christ in the world, whose individual members are called to manifest his Spirit in all of life. The Church must be the leaven which permeates all of society with its message.

There are, of course, many problems connected with the implementation of our call from God in our sub-Christian world. In the realm of daily work, perhaps more than in any other, there are seemingly insurmountable problems. There is a vast difference in the way in which work is carried on in our technological age and in the manner in which the craftsman labored in the Middle Ages, where each person often saw an article through from raw material to finished product. There are countless jobs that must be done in which it is difficult to find meaning. Many types of work are monotonous or mean, and the manner of acting as a Christian in many types of work is difficult, so difficult, in fact, that many people cease trying to find meaning in work and seek it in other realms of life.[16]

In other areas, many problems also exist. How does one live as a Christian in politics? In social life? In his community relationships? In the various clubs and organizations to which he belongs? Which ones will he join and which will he shun? How can he work alongside non-Christians when the cause seems just, even though his motivation is different from that of the person with whom he works? These and many other questions demand more adequate and clearer thinking than is usually given them in the Church today.

There is the further problem in fulfilling one's vocation in the world —that of communication to those outside the Church. As we shall later see, much of the language of the Church today is either rejected or misunderstood by modern man. The temptation for the Christian is either to use the same old pious terms, and have them either rejected or effectively ignored, or else not to speak as a Christian at all. One of the problems of our age, as of every age, is how to make the gospel relevant. We cannot adequately fulfill our call from God except as we find ways of putting the age-old gospel in terms which can be understood and become meaningful to modern man.

While these and other related questions are not easily answered, it is imperative that the sensitive Christian search for answers. For if the Church is to be made alive in our world today, means must be found whereby the vocation of being a Christian can be expressed in the various orders of society. This may even mean that the church as an institution will seem to cease to prosper, for if this concept is taken seriously the primary function of the local church may become that of training the layman to exercise his vocation *outside* the walls of the church. The Church, like the individual, may have to lose its life in order to find its life. The Church alive in the world is the Church witnessing to its Lord and Master however this may best take place.

This exercising of one's vocation in the various orders of society is neither easy nor spectacular. Indeed it is only through a slow, loving process that it can take place. For example, one of the most difficult groups to touch may be organized labor. The *organized* church may not be able to reach organized labor at all, but it is likely that individual Christians can infiltrate local groups and make their witness, not through pious cant but rather through a daily witness of love and concern for neighbor.

The same thing can be said of all "secular" organizations: the social fraternity on the college campus, the professional society, the businessman's organization, the public school, social agencies, youth groups, and a host of others. The object must not be to further one's own particular church, nor to use one's official position to win converts. For example, the public school teacher cannot be an evangelist through actually seeking to win adherents to a particular faith. Yet the teacher can be an evangelist through the quality of life he lives, the relationships he maintains, the type of ministry he performs in meeting the needs of children and confused teen-agers. All of this is difficult and the way in which it is to be done is only partially known. If the early Christians could, by being "saints in Caesar's household," win others to the Christ, then there is hope that we can do so likewise.

The problem of living as a Christian in our sub-Christian society is not an easy one to meet. Yet each Christian's vocation is to do no less than this. Man is called to serve God *and* his fellow men, regardless of his occupation. Further, if the Church is to be a dynamic fellowship in which children can be nurtured and which can witness to the world concerning the reality of the gospel, those who compose the fellowship must take their calling seriously. Nothing less than this can answer the needs of life today.

PART II

THE MISSION OF THE LAITY

VI

The Church as a Worshiping Community

THUS FAR WE HAVE BEEN CONCERNED PRIMARILY WITH THE NATURE of the Church—its existence as the Body of Christ in the world and the response of those called to be members of his Body. The insistence has been made that how the Church *acts* ought to be rooted and grounded in what the Church *is,* and further that to understand the character of its mission we must first be aware of its nature as a gift of God to man, thus recognizing that it is more than an institution of man's contriving.

We are ready now to turn to the manner in which the Church expresses itself in the world. No attempt is made to be complete in this discussion, since several of the ministries of the Church are omitted almost completely. For example, no reference is made directly to the area of pastoral care and counseling and only incidental references are made to preaching. These are considered as more directly the responsibility of the ordained and trained minister, and thus are omitted as part of the consideration of the more universal ministry of the Church through teaching and nurture, group life, outreach, and administration. There are, of course, lay preachers and lay counselors, and surely personal visitation and counseling are involved in teaching, group life, outreach, and administration.

Before we turn to these more easily identifiable "functions," however, we must discuss a concept which serves as a bridge between our consideration of the *nature* of the Church and that of its *mission.* Worship, our immediate interest, is very close to the heart of the meaning of the Church itself; yet it is also its primary office or "function." The Church *is* a worshiping community or it is simply *not* the Church, while, at the same time the first and foremost response of the persons involved in the Church is worship. Traditional definitions of the Church recognize this when it is defined as "a congregation of faithful men in which the pure Word of God is preached, and the Sacraments duly administered according to Christ's ordinance." [1] It is to an attempt to understand the Church as a worshiping community that we now turn.

71

Man's Call to Worship

We have said (in Chap. V) that God's call to man is for him to act responsibly in the totality of his existence. This involves *all* kinds of service to God, including that rendered to our fellow men and through them to God. The cup of water given in Christ's name (Spirit) is given to him (Matt. 25:40). But service also involves the response of man in worship of God.

This point of view is somewhat difficult for activist Christians in America to understand, however. We have taken quite literally I John 3:17: "But if any one has the world's goods and sees his brother in need, yet closes his heart against him, how does God's love abide in him?" At least in theory we have taken this statement seriously however far short we have fallen in practice. Abou ben Adhem[2] has been made the ideal of the Christian who wants to be considered as one who loves the Lord, and we have found it almost impossible to say with John Milton, "They also serve who only stand and wait." [3]

Without question the New Testament is clear that service to God which ignores one's brother is empty and meaningless. It is equally clear, however, that service without the motivation which consists in the person's response to God is sub-Christian. "If I give away all I have, and if I deliver my body to be burned, but have not love, I gain nothing" (I Cor. 13:3). It seems reasonably clear that the kind of love (*agape*) about which Paul is writing here is deeper than that motivated by purely humanitarian reasons. The inevitable result of a service-centered theology that is primarily humanitarian in its basis would seem to be something like that which happened to nineteenth- and early twentieth-century Liberalism: it tended to become a new legalism, not in the keeping of negative rules so much as in the earning of one's salvation through acts of good will. Also, from a purely practical point of view, a benevolence which is founded on such motivation is likely to deteriorate in time; we cannot forever enjoy the fruits of faith without its roots.

Previous chapters in this work should have made it clear that no such humanitarian-based religion is considered adequate to meet the needs of the day nor is it in harmony with the basic Christian faith. We have tried to say that man's basic response is to God, and that there flow from this response attitudes of love and acts of service to our fellow men. We are at a point now where we need a clearer interpretation of what service to God is, however. This we must do by considering the central act of the Church as a corporate fellowship (and, of course, the central response of the individual), namely, the worship of God.

We have repeatedly spoken of the secularization of the Church, of its failure to be the community of faith, the Body of Christ, the People of God. Thus from two points of view a renewed emphasis on worship seems mandatory: first, that the Church may really be the Church since its very nature demands such a response, and second, that some practical means may be found whereby the renewal of the Church might begin. Such a renewal must spring from a greater emphasis on the central response of the Church, that from which all others must originate: the worship of almighty God.

Indeed, until this emphasis is made central, it is quite likely that churches will continue to be more like social clubs than units of the Body of Christ. Our local churches must cease being centered about the kitchen and return to the altar. This is not to say that eating together is not important—there is a profound significance in the experience of the two followers of Jesus who walked with the risen Christ on the road to Emmaus: "He was known to them in the breaking of bread" (Luke 24:35). But the breaking of bread in the church is likely to lose its symbolic significance unless the life of worship of the congregation is rich and dynamic.

Service to God and worship of God are very closely related to one another in the New Testament, and a discussion of one involves a discussion of the other. This close connection has come to us in a way which we usually ignore: namely, in the fact that we still speak of *services* of worship, or a worship *service*. Although it can be argued that the typical evangelical service is more of a *show* than a *service*, the fact remains that the connection between worship and service has persisted even if the meaning behind it may have been lost.

This close connection between worship and service may be illustrated by the difficulty which translators find in rendering Rom. 12:1. The King James Version translates the final phrase, "which is your reasonable service"; the American Standard Version renders it, "which is your spiritual service"; and the Revised Standard Version translates the same phrase, "which is your spiritual worship." Goodspeed retains "worship" by translating the phrase, "that is your rational worship," while Moffatt has the phrase read, "that is your cult, a spiritual rite."

In other words, the Greek word *latreia* may actually be translated into both "service" and "worship," with the lexicons often giving such definitions as "to serve, especially to worship." Perhaps the statement may be paraphrased in this means: "The offering of one's *self* to God is the only adequate way of worshiping God." [4] Or as John Knox has put it: "The meaning may be, 'This worship is appropriate to your new spiritual life'; or it may be, 'This worship is really God's Spirit offering your worship for you.'" [5]

Eph. 6:7 further indicates that service must always be to God, not primarily to man: ". . . rendering service with a good will as to the Lord and not to men." Service, then, is rendering back to God that which is due him—it is the thing we ought to do because of our very dependence on God. To put it another way, the Christian serves that which is worthful, and this is God. Since the word "worship" actually comes from an Anglo-Saxon one meaning "worthful," [6] the connection between worship and service is again indicated.

Another way of illustrating this close relationship between worship and service is to look at the meaning of the word "liturgy." In modern usage this word is most often used to describe worship that follows a set form, with a fairly fixed order, using prayers that are prescribed, with certain parts of the service either said or chanted by the priest and others said or chanted by people and priest together. In other words, it is equated with *ritualism,* and in some churches emphasizing a freer form of worship liturgical worship is anathema.

The original Greek word, *leitourgia,* from which liturgy derives, has quite a different meaning, however. There are two primary meanings: first, service to the state *voluntarily* assumed, and second, service *laid upon* the citizen who was particularly capable of rendering some service. As used in the New Testament, it applies to service rendered by man to man, service done before God (even the high priestly work of Christ himself in Heb. 8:6, 8:2), and service laid upon the Christian to be an evangelist to others (Rom. 15:16).[7]

Thus, as Dom Gregory Dix so well points out, "liturgy" historically was applied to something *done*. When used to signify worship, it was people *and* priest together offering themselves to God, and thus it referred directly to service done before God.[8] J. Ernest Rattenbury, in his excellent work on the Eucharistic hymns of the Wesleys, has summarized Dix's position in this manner:

The Greek word from which it [liturgy] is derived means "active service," and it was used to describe the actions—the corporate actions—of the Church. The Liturgy was not the work of a priest who said a Mass for people to listen to, or, when said in a foreign language, showed them a wafer to gaze upon. It was something everybody did. Liturgy was service, not in a literary sense, but in an active sense. Every member of the congregation where the Eucharistic sacrifice was offered was not only a worshipper but an offerer.[9]

What is said here is meant neither to identify service to follow men with worship nor to disparage the importance of such service. Rather it is to indicate that public worship and daily life are intimately associated and that the two must be seen in relation to one another if we are to fulfill our call from God to service. Our primary service to God is in worship offered before him; flowing from that service is that which we render to him through acts of benevolence toward our fellow men. This, of course, is in harmony with the order in which Jesus quoted the two summaries of the Law from the Old Testament: Love God, *and* your neighbor. (Matt. 22:37-39; Mark 12:30-31; Luke 10:27.)

Although in one sense all of the life lived in obedience to God is lived in the spirit of worship, there is obviously a need for special acts of worship. Further, although personal worship and private prayers are essential for living responsively before God, there is a distinctive quality to public worship. It is the Church as a fellowship offering itself before God. Moreover, in these special acts of worship the drama of redemption is made known to us again and we worship him who is the author of redemption.

"Subjective-Objective" Aspects of Worship

What has been said thus far indicates that worship is an act of a congregation offering itself up before God. The central facts of worship are God and man's response to God. What happens to man as a result of this act is not unimportant, but it *is* derivative. To be worship rather than an aesthetic or purely emotional experience, worship must be centered on that which is worthful. The fact of the matter, however, is that much that goes under the name of worship in the modern church is often more concerned with creating a mood, producing a good feeling, inspiring action, than it is with praising God. It is this aspect of worship that has received the attention of psychologists, since it can, to some extent, be measured, tested, and described.

This emphasis is what James B. Pratt in his book published a number of years ago called the "subjective" aspects of worship. It was his contention that Protestant worship tends to be primarily "subjective" while Roman Catholic worship is primarily "objective," that is, aimed toward the object of worship with little consideration for the subjective response on the part of the worshiper.[10] While recognizing that these words are used in a somewhat different manner in modern theology and thus that it is easy for Pratt's meaning to be obscured,[11] it would seem appropriate still to point to this distinction which he made. It is true, of course, that modern philosophy and theology have helped us see that there cannot be as radical a distinction between subject and object as Pratt's distinction might seem to indicate.

As proof of the fact that this "subjective" aspect of worship is the one most recognized by Protestants, one need only ask a group of people to name their most worshipful experience. (Even the question, of course, implies the feeling side of worship, and may not be a proper question.) In most groups many will name a vesper service, a candle-light service, a service under unusual circumstances like sitting on a hilltop at sunset or watching a burning cross across the lake. In other words the emphasis is put on the reaction of the participant, the exalted feeling or emotional uplift which he experiences, which may or may not have anything to do with the God and Father of our Lord Jesus Christ. Perhaps the failure is not really that there is *no* object of worship but rather that the object which the subject is led to center on is something other than God.

This type of worship, especially popular in youth meetings during recent years, emphasizing sunsets and sunrises, bonfires and candles, tall trees and placid lakes, led the editors of *Christianity and Crisis* to announce recently the discovery of a new religion which they call naturism. With a certain tongue-in-cheek attitude they wrote:

At this time of year, in places where there are cool breezes, mountain vistas, forest glades, sylvan lakes (how easily the phrases come to mind!) or even inviting fairways, the adherents of Naturism begin to go on a spree. . . . The gods of Naturism usually receive homage at the interfaith gatherings known as Summer Conferences. At such places there is usually a Cathedral of the Pines, in which worshipers are directed to meditate upon the beauty and straightness of trees rather than upon the Creator of the trees. At such places there is always an Inspiration Point. . . . You will be particularly conscious of this if you come to it right after hearing an "inspirational address" by a "denominational leader." [12]

Now one need not reject completely the atmosphere of the out-of-doors as a fitting place for worship in order to see that the symbols of modern worship are in danger of becoming objects of nature rather than the Cross and other traditional Christian symbols. How often the words of the poem, "You are nearer to God in a garden than anywhere else on earth," have been repeated at such "nature services" would be difficult to determine!

This same concern for the superficiality of much modern worship led J. Ernest Rattenbury, the British Methodist, to write in the preface to his book on worship:

I am convinced that the disease from which much of our worship suffers is organic rather than functional, and that no reform of Liturgy, however wisely devised to deal with symptoms, will of itself solve the problem. What is needed primarily is an examination of the causes of the unsatisfying character of many of our religious services. Hence this book while encouraging Liturgical reform and making practical suggestions toward it, is much more concerned with underlying principles and problems. I most of all plead in the following pages for the restoration of "objectivity" to Free Church and particularly to Methodist worship. My strong conviction is that our emphasis on the value of subjective and individualistic worship, necessary as it has been as a protest against the ceremonialism and rigidity of "Catholic" ritual, has gone too far and that to-day a restoration of certain neglected corporate and historical elements of devotion in our public services is essential for truly balanced Christian worship.[13]

There are signs that youth leaders are among those who recognize the trap into which their special types of worship services have led them. For example, Roger Ortmayer, editor of the Methodist college students' magazine *motive*, reported a renewed concern for traditional worship at the Fifth Quadrennial Conference of the Methodist Student Movement held at the beginning of 1954. After pointing out that worship was a prominent feature of the conference and was conducted according to forms taken from various traditions, he went on to say: "It demonstrated that the Methodist Student Movement must stimulate more conversation on the *meaning* of worship, that the day of pleas for enriching worship is gone. . . . Interestingly," he continued, "Methodist student groups today are more prone to be split by disagreement over worship than over social issues." [14]

This part of our topic has been considered at some length because it seems of crucial importance for a deeper understanding of the meaning of public worship and its significance in the Christian faith community. It should be emphasized, moreover, that nothing that has been said is intended to imply that the response of the worshiper— his feelings, his "subjective" experience—is not important. Those who fear liturgical forms are right in their allegations that they *may* become empty and meaningless to the worshiper, though it is the contention here that, when understood, they may also become a means for enriching the response of the worshiper. Loving and worshiping God with heart, mind, soul, and strength implies a total response of knowing, feeling, and doing.

This means, for example, that we are right in providing experiences of worship *graded* for a child's capacity to respond, though we are equally justified in insisting that children, at least by eight or nine years of age and probably younger, ought to participate in corporate Sunday worship even though they are not able to understand its full meaning. It is imperative that boys and girls at the earliest practicable age shall begin to recognize themselves as part of a worshiping community which includes adults as well as children. We are correct, also, in insisting that one of the "moods" of worship is offering, or commitment, and thus we will not be unmindful of the importance of creating a service that evokes from the worshiper a response of offering, commitment, and rededication. We are equally obliged, however, to attempt to make clear that the *object* of worship is almighty God and that a service of worship is a *corporate* act, not the individual devotions of a group of people who happen to be together in the same room.

Corporate Worship

The word *corporate*, indeed, is the key word for our consideration of the meaning of public worship. Our failure to make of our morning services corporate experiences reminds us again of the strong individualism which has characterized evangelical Protestantism, especially during the last century. A worshiping congregation *is* more than a collection of individuals carrying on their private devotions. Rather, it ought to be a *body* of Christians offering themselves *as a body* as well as individually to God, led by an ordained minister who serves in the capacity of officiant, not mediator.

It is interesting to note how this concept has survived even in non-ritualistic worship. For example, the familiar phrase, "We will now be *led* in prayer by Brother Jones," is reminiscent of the time when the congregation prayed together either vocally or under the leadership of one person actually speaking the words. Unfortunately in practice Brother Jones is more likely to give a discourse *to* the congregation than to pray to God *with* the congregation.

Thus, a point at which we can focus our thinking with respect to public worship is a recurring theme of this book: the *koinonia* as the heart of the meaning of the Church. In Chap. IV it was pointed out that unmistakably the fellowship of the early Church was not only with one another but also, perhaps primarily, with Christ. The Spirit pervaded the fellowship, indeed made it possible. The Body of Christ had been called into being by the action of God in Jesus Christ, and the Spirit continued as the sustaining power of the Body. What would be more natural than for the people of God to consider their principal response to God who had so acted to be worship? "And day by day, attending the temple together and breaking bread in their homes, they partook of food with glad and generous hearts, praising God and having favor with all the people." (Acts 2:46-47*a*.)

A service of worship, then, is a re-enactment of the drama of redemption not by a group of players (minister, choir, organist) for the congregation to watch what is done, but rather by a congregation, *including* minister, choir, and organist, every person being an actor in the drama. True liturgical worship is just this: a congregation in fellowship with God and with one another, offering *themselves* (not bread and wine, or a lovely solo, or an anthem well performed, or even a sermon however convicting it may be) in thanksgiving, confession, praise, and commitment to God. Symbols, such as bread and wine, water, anthem, the reading of the Holy Scriptures, the praying of corporate prayers, the sermon, are means through which the congregation expresses itself. This is a *corporate* act: it emerges out of the fellowship and at the same time it makes fellowship possible. It is significant that at a time when Protestantism is rediscovering historic ritual as a means of corporate worship, Roman Catholicism through the liturgical movement is rediscovering the significance of the people as real participants in the Mass.[15]

As was indicated in the citation from Rattenbury, this understanding of worship as a corporate act will result in something quite different from what has commonly been done through the "enriching" of worship. George MacLeod, of the Iona Community, has described the loss of worship in Scotland and the consequent attempt to improve the situation. "The Church that feared the muse, now openly advertises the soloist," he writes. "And, short of 'electric preaching,' or 'a really forceful young man in the pulpit,' congregations—whether they indulge these 'little innovations' or spartanly deny them—are becoming dimly conscious that an ending is in sight." [16]

In other words, no efforts at introducing chants, or adding a printed prayer here or there, or the providing of a printed order of service, or any other such effort of shoring up present practices, will suffice. In fact, such "appurtenances" (if such they be) may be out of place in the total setting and with the present understanding of the people. It is no solution for the Methodists to imitate the Episcopalians and the Episcopalians to imitate the Romans, though it *is* possible to learn from each other and to borrow elements of liturgy from the various traditions, provided they are meaningful.

Toward a Reconsideration of Worship

This is not to deny the necessity for the improvement of worship as it is now practiced in a particular local church or in a denomination. Such improvement may become the means both for the congregation's becoming more aware of itself as a corporate body and for its coming to understand more fully the meaning and significance of worship. The appearance of books of worship (as for example one of the more recent, that published for the Disciples of Christ, *Christian Worship: A Service Book*),[17] is to be commended. For many local congregations improvement will involve such elemental matters as seeking to establish proper conduct in the house of worship, the provision of a more complete order of service (including confession; praise, testimony and witness; petition; offering and commitment),[18] the introduction of better hymns more appropriately used, the return to more reading of the Bible in the service, and other similar changes. Other local congregations may be ready for the adoption of traditional worship forms. For example, many Methodist churches, which have already gone through part or all of the more elementary phases, may now be ready to take seriously that church's *Book of Worship*, which contains most of the historical elements of worship,[19] and such is true of other evangelical churches possessing a liturgical tradition but not now fully utilizing it.

As we have said, however, it is not enough simply to improve or enrich our services of worship. Understanding of what is done must accompany such improvement. A minister who himself comes to understand the meaning of worship and to appreciate its forms of expression has taken this step in his own thinking. Now he must share this insight with his congregation. In other words, the education of a congregation in worship is imperative.

One student minister, who had himself come to appreciate more fully the nature and significance of corporate worship, has recounted how he helped his congregation through this experience.[20] Since the church was in the process of building a new church building, an added inducement was given for the congregation to prepare itself for the new building. For a year prior to the completion of the building, this student pastor had taken every opportunity to acquaint his parishioners with the meaning of worship. Sermons, Wednesday evening "prayer meetings," and other occasions were utilized for this process. In the meantime, step by step, he was introducing into the order of worship elements to make it more complete. On the Sunday prior to the opening of the new church building, the completed order of service was presented to the congregation through an explanation of each element in the service prior to its use. Instead of a separate sermon, the sermon of this morning consisted of a presentation at the various points of the service of the reasons for the inclusion of that part. When the first service was held in the new church, the congregation was then ready to participate fully and gladly in the expanded service of worship.

Further, while this reconsideration of worship will involve a return to historic forms, it ought also to include experimentation in both new forms and language. It is dangerous to experiment, yet necessary. This is not to suggest entirely new forms, for the Christian community as it now exists has a history of more than nineteen centuries and to ignore this history is to suggest that the Spirit has been inactive during those centuries. But what about the language of worship? Is it possible that thought forms have changed sufficiently that this necessitates some radical changes? It is true that even a radical biblical scholar like Rudolf Bultmann, who feels that the gospel must be "demythologized" in order that it can be heard in today's world outside the Church, does

81

not agree that the language of worship (that is, the language used *inside* the Christian community) needs such a revision.[21] Similarly, Karl Barth insists that whereas the language in which the gospel is communicated to the world must be modern, that used within the faith Community ought to follow the terminology and the symbolism inherent within the historic language of faith.[22] Yet not to bring the language of worship into relative harmony with the language of preaching, teaching, and evangelism would seem to make worship too far removed from the experiences of everyday life.

Similarly, experimentation must be carried on in church architecture, symbolism, and other "outward and visible signs" of worship so that they can become real means of "inward grace" to modern man. Fortunately, the revival of Gothic and other medieval and colonial forms of church architecture seems to have abated, and the increasing number of churches employing contemporary architectural principles and forms is heartening. There is still, however, the need for architectural forms which express the spirit of this age as well as Gothic and other forms expressed the spirit of bygone ages. Further, the trend to an elevated altar in evangelical churches is being called into question, and the communion table is being moved away from the back of the chancel to the so-called basilican position, into the center of the chancel. This is not to suggest the return to the central pulpit, of course, which places the preacher, not the Table, at the center. But the central Table-Altar, rather than the raised altar, does seem more in harmony with evangelical Protestantism.[23]

The aim of such creative efforts in worship is twofold: first, to seek to make the Church really a worshiping community, with a real *service of worship* (or liturgy) offered by *all* the people, and second, to bring worship into a relationship to office and market place so that liturgy again refers to an act of offering which is real and vital, not something which is gone through as a matter of form. It should be noted that these reforms are fully as important for those churches not now utilizing historic forms as it is for those employing such forms. The ritual (for there is always some kind of ritual, however unhistoric it may be) for the "free" churches is often as unrelated to life generally as is the language of many of the historic forms, and it suffers the additional weakness of having no precedent within the Christian community. The language patterns in which persons offer "extemporaneous" prayers in church services are often quite meaningless. The songs used in "gospel meetings" are frequently quite irrelevant so far as life is concerned. A good example is the popular gospel song, "In the Garden." Try relating the words of that song to the life of the typical member of the Men's Bible Class, which often sings it!

What we have said is that in this revival of worship we should neither ignore the historic past nor be enslaved to it. Having recognized this freedom, it is quite likely that we shall find in the forms of the historic Church that which also expresses *our* thanksgiving, *our* confession, *our* praise, *our* commitment, *our* decision. Whatever form is used, however, it ought to be such as to encourage the sense of participation as a member of a corporate body.

Nothing that is said concerning the importance of an increased emphasis on worship is intended to deny the significance of preaching in Protestantism. Ilion Jones is right when he calls into question the tendency by some modern ministers to deny the importance of the sermon in worship.[24] The *preached* word, along with the *read* word from Scripture, is a necessary part of Christian worship. This was the case in early worship, and the omission of the sermon or the tendency to make it unimportant in later times is not true to historic forms of worship. The recovery of the preached word by the reformers must not be lost by modern Protestantism. Actually, however, if the total service of worship is understood—with one large section being devoted to testimony, praise, and instruction—this need not be the case at all. Indeed, a recovery of worship might well remind the preacher of the fact that the pulpit is not a lecture platform and thus he might be led to take more seriously his task of proclaiming the Word of God through a recounting of the life, death, and resurrection of Jesus Christ, and its meaning for modern man.[25]

The Sacrament of Baptism

If the Church is to take itself in all seriousness as the Body of Christ, it must also reaffirm its sacramental nature. This is not to suggest *sacerdotalism*: that is, a return to the medieval practice whereby the keys of the Kingdom are entrusted to priests. It is to say that the Church must, in all seriousness, reconsider the meaning of baptism and the Lord's Supper, or Holy Communion.

Both of these sacraments tend to be taken lightly by many churchmen, both clergy and laity. The Sacrament of Holy Communion has in many local congregations been relegated to a place of insignificance, being held infrequently in the regular morning service, perhaps somewhat more frequently in the chapel or at a special "vesper" service. Far too often this service, which was the heart of Christian worship from New Testament times until fairly recently, is treated with embarrassment, as if it were something that has to be done occasionally just to keep up appearances. In some churches, either because the laity does not understand the significance of the service or because the minister has not made it seem important, it can be expected that attendance at a Communion service will be smaller than that at a regular "preaching service." As for baptism, it is often not understood, is administered in a perfunctory manner, and is treated as if it too were of little importance.

Let us look first at baptism as related to worship. Because different meanings are put on this rite by various communions, one discusses it with trepidation. Since this has already been discussed with respect to its relationship to the meaning of the Church,[26] it will be treated here primarily as it relates to worship.

Whatever may be the practice of a particular denomination, the service of baptism, whether it be for infants or for adults, ought to be an opportunity for the re-enactment of the drama of redemption. In baptism, the Church, through its ordained ministry but with the corporate body participating, performs a sign which signifies that something is done for the person that he cannot do for himself. It is, in a real sense, the symbol of God's redeeming love as manifested in Jesus Christ. He is received into Christ's holy flock not by virtue of an act on his part—that is confirmation, or the assuming of the covenantal relationship for himself—but by virtue of God's grace, mediated through the Church. It is, whether the person is unable at all to assume personal responsibility as in the case of an infant, or whether he is, as an adult, ready to accept the responsibility of an immature member of the fellowship through immediate confirmation, the assuming by the Church of its responsibility for the nurture of that person. Thus it ought to be a high and holy moment in the life of the fellowship, with the congregation participating with the parents of the child or with the adults involved. The time at which the person himself assumes the vows of the covenantal relationship ought also to be a solemn occasion, whether this immediately follows baptism as in the case of an adult, or whether several years elapse as in the case of a person who is baptized in infancy.

This will probably mean that these ceremonies ought not to be carried out at the end of each service, as they are in many evangelical churches. To be sure, part of the genius of evangelical Protestantism is the opportunity which is given at the end of each service for persons in the congregation to make a decision for their life's destiny. If we believe that the Holy Spirit works through our services of worship to convict and convince, then we must give persons the opportunity of making their decision a matter of record. This does not mean, however, that services of baptism and reception into church membership need be held at the end of each service, when very often they are gone through in a perfunctory manner. Having presented himself publicly to the congregation as an applicant for baptism or church membership, the applicant then ought to be given a period of training in the meaning of the decision he has reached. Following such instruction, he will then be baptized and received into membership on some stated occasion, in a service that is dignified, unhurried, worshipful, and fitting to the seriousness of the occasion. No wonder that church membership is so little thought of by many church members when, as someone has put it, it is easier to join a church than to board a bus!

The Sacrament of Holy Communion

If baptism is the symbol of the acceptance by God of the person in the first instance, Holy Communion is the assurance of his continued acceptance. It is no wonder that a church that has become an instrument of moral uplift for the community should be embarrassed by the ancient rite of the Eucharist (thanksgiving), for it speaks of things far deeper than simply "being good." Rather, it speaks to us of the evil in men's hearts after baptism and regeneration and the need for a regular reminder of the saving love of God as manifest in the death, burial, and resurrection of Jesus Christ. It is the heart of the *koinonia* (communion) of which we have spoken in previous chapters. No wonder, then, that John Wesley put so much emphasis on the service of Communion, attending himself at least once a week and advising his followers to do also, for in his day, as in ours, attendance at Communion had fallen disgracefully low.[27]

What then is the meaning of the Lord's Supper? Obviously all we

85

can do here is to point to its meanings,[28] since it is far too rich to be considered in such a short space.

It is first of all (though this may not be its *primary* meaning) a memorial: "Do this in remembrance of me" (I Cor. 11:24). Modern man can understand this meaning of the service rather easily, but he often stops short even of the full significance of this aspect. As Olive Wyon has pointed out, "memorial" is actually not a good word to describe this aspect of the rite. The Greek word, *anamnesis,* she reminds us, actually means "a calling to mind." "When we 'call to mind' an event which means a great deal to us we think of it with all its associations." [29] This recalling, she goes on to show, "means that something 'past' becomes 'present,' something which, here and now, affects us vitally and profoundly. In other words, 'the Eucharist is the "memorial"—that is, the *anamnesis,* the making present—of the true Paschal Lamb who is the Christ.' " [30] Every celebration reminds us, then, that our faith is based on historic fact, and this historic fact becomes a present reality to us.[31] This is something of what "the real Presence" can mean to the person who does not believe that any physical change takes place in the elements.

This leads to two further meanings of the Supper: for one thing, it is a means of proclaiming Christ's death, or to put it more broadly, it is the re-enactment of the death and resurrection of our Lord, not in the sense that the event is repeated but rather in the sense that it is dramatized. "For as often as you eat this bread and drink the cup, you proclaim the Lord's death until he comes." (I Cor. 11:26.)

Also, this reminds us of a third meaning: not only does the celebration *proclaim;* it allows us to *participate,* to *commune.* "The cup of blessing which we bless, is it not a participation in the blood of Christ? The bread which we break, is it not a participation in the body of Christ?" (I Cor. 10:16.) This, according to Rudolf Bultmann, was the central meaning of the Communion meal in the New Testament.[32] We take part in the central affirmation of the Christian faith, the atonement through Christ. Thus Christ's presence becomes *real* to us through the action of the Holy Spirit.

Further, this is an act of repentance on the part of the participant. "This is my blood of the covenant, which is poured out for many for the forgiveness of sins." (Matt. 26:28.) "We do earnestly repent, and are heartily sorry for these our misdoings"—so runs the Prayer of General Confession.

Also, it is an act of rededication. "And here we offer and present unto thee, O Lord, ourselves, our souls and bodies, to be a reasonable, holy, and living sacrifice unto thee, humbly beseeching thee that all we who are partakers of this Holy Communion may be filled with thy grace and heavenly benediction." [33]

Finally, overarching all of these meanings is one which resulted in one of the early names given to the celebration "Eucharist," or thanksgiving. The service commemorates the death of Jesus, to be sure, but it also points to the triumphant quality of this death. It reminds the participant of the continuing love of God to him, made known dramatically and uniquely in the sacrifice of Christ but ever-present through the continuing activity of God in the Holy Spirit. This is caught up in the ancient hymn of praise, which, though coming early in most ancient services and restored to this place in the new ritual of the Church of South India, comes at the end of the service for churches following the English tradition. "We praise thee, we bless thee, we worship thee, we glorify thee, we give thanks to thee for thy great glory, O Lord God, heavenly King, God the Father Almighty!"

With these aspects of the service in mind, it is easy to see how it has been, and may be again, the central act of worship of the Church. Perhaps it need not be thought of as the *norm* for public worship, so that, in a sense, all other services of worship are less than this one. Yet there is considerable feeling present in the Church today that those churches which have largely neglected it within recent years ought again to place it in its rightful place of centrality in the Church. Both to be true to its heritage and to unite the congregation in an act of communion around the Lord's table, with one another and with God, the centrality of Holy Communion must be reasserted.

Worship and Koinonia

It may appear that this somewhat extensive discourse on the meaning of worship has led us away from our central theme: the Church as the Body of Christ and a redemptive fellowship. Yet, if the central act of such a fellowship is service to God that centers in worship, this is not the case. Further, perhaps the weakest point of many parish churches is their failure to educate their members in and lead them to share in meaningful services of worship. Thus, purely from the instrumental view, a return to worship is essential. Such worship ought to be liturgical in the best sense of the word in that it becomes a common

87

offering of a corporate body. Further, it ought to be so related to the common life of the people that work and worship are seen as complementary means of offering one's self to God. Special acts of worship should lift up the concerns, the problems, the thanksgiving, the confessions, the petitions of a congregation in such a manner that cathedral and market place are brought into relevance one to another and all of life is united around one common theme. Only then will the injunction of Paul be realized: "I appeal to you therefore, brethren, by the mercies of God, to present your bodies as a living sacrifice, holy and acceptable to God, which is your spiritual worship." (Rom. 12:1.)

VII

Nurturing Life Within the Christian Community

IN ORDER FOR THE CHURCH TO EXIST, IT MUST BE A WORSHIPING community in which the Sacraments are duly administered. In Protestantism, preaching is also considered normative for the existence of the Church.[1] Beyond these two offices, there is disagreement concerning the importance and the nature of other ministries. One which is widely recognized, though sometimes neglected, is teaching, or in its broader definition, nurture. As James Smart has put it, "The Church must teach, just as it must preach, or it will not be the Church. . . . Teaching belongs to the essence of the Church and a church that neglects this function of teaching has lost something that is indispensable to its nature as a church."[2]

It is to this office that we now turn our attention with no expectation of being able to provide an adequate presentation of it. Rather, the purpose is to state a philosophy of Christian nurture consistent with the view of the Church presented in earlier chapters.

Christian Nurture and the Church

The *first* assertion that may be made concerning Christian nurture is this: *it takes place within the Christian community (Church) as it exists in the family, in the organized church, and in other groups* which, though not actually called the church, bring into being the relationships which have true Christian meaning. It is possible to teach *about* religion in the public schools; there may be a residual kind of Christian faith inherent in such groups as the Boy Scouts, fraternal organizations, and various clubs; but only as the quality of life of any group reaches a consciously Christian level does Christian nurture occur. This may even be said about the organized church.

Much that was said in earlier chapters is closely related to this basic assertion. We have repeatedly said that life is lived in fellowship, that there is no such thing as an isolated being, that the Christian faith is social by its very nature. The human self is "called into being" as one individual responds to other selves. What we are at any given time must be seen both in terms of our present actual existence and our potential existence. Whether or not the self that emerges is organized in a Christian manner thus depends on the quality of relationships which that self has enjoyed. The emergence of the self related to the eternal "Thou" is dependent upon the type of relationships between human "thous." Christian nurture occurs as the self is related to other selves in a Christian community. And the self is always a growing self: "Beloved, we are God's children now; it does not yet appear what we shall be, but we know that when he appears we shall be like him, for we shall see him as he is" (I John 3:2).

All of this implies that a *program* of Christian teaching must be *Church-centered* in the sense that it must be fundamentally the Church at work in the nurture of children, youth, and adults. In the earlier years of the modern religious education movement (that is, the movement which flowered in the early twentieth century under Coe, Bower, Elliott, and others), religious education was sometimes divorced from the organized church because a theology not consonant with that of the Church was set up for the educational program. There are still examples of programs of education which, though used by the Church, are not Church centered. For example, the Character Research Project, carried on under the leadership of Ernest Ligon, tends to be separate from the ongoing life of the church, even though it may be adapted to different churches. Whenever a program of education does not begin with the theologizing of and about the Church, it runs the risk of being sub-Christian.

Indeed, another way of stating this is that Christian nurture must take as its beginning point the theological thinking of the Church, not general education. This does not mean that the insights of psychology and general education cannot be used by the Church. It does insist that Christian nurture must begin with theology, not conceived as a static system, but rather as a dynamic expression of faith.[3] Christian nurture occurs wherever the Church is at work leading persons into a dynamic encounter with the Lord of the Church.

Christian Nurture and Learning

The *second* major assertion that we must make is that *learning is a process involving the total spectrum of influences that make a person*

90

what he is. Learning (and thus teaching) in the Church is a much broader enterprise than we have sometimes believed.

Often the teaching function of the Church is defined as the deliberate and conscious effort to impart facts, ideas, and attitudes, *TRANS-MISSIVE* its purpose being to lead to conduct which is in keeping with the ethics of the New Testament. If Christian teaching could be confined to such planned situations, the task would be relatively simple. If boys and girls learned only what adults wanted them to learn, a race of super-adults might result. But such is not the case, for teaching goes on continually in all human communities; and the Church, as we have already asserted, teaches more by what it does than by what it says, and even more by what it is than what it does.[4] The same statement can, of course, be made with respect to the family.

To appreciate the significance of this truth, we need to review briefly the modern understanding of the learning process. Learning is continuous, occurring both through the conscious and unconscious influence of one person upon another. True, one of the fundamental ways of learning is through *trial and error*, which implies a certain *(1)* independence from other human persons. A young child learns much simply by ascertaining in the everyday process of living what works and what does not. Primitive man also learned much through trying and either discarding or accepting. Further, independent thinking, such as Dewey described in *How We Think,* involves a kind of trial and error as one arrives at a hypothesis and tests out the hypothesis.

A child does not begin with a neutral environment, however; rather, he comes into a society which already has skills, knowledge, attitudes, *cau* and corporate feelings. Therefore much of his learning occurs through what we call *conditioning,* a process which has received considerable *(2)* empirical verification in experiments beginning with Pavlof. In this process an animal or a human person comes to respond automatically to a particular stimulus in a particular manner.

It is obvious that all of us, but especially children, are conditioned to respond to many common stimuli in life. Whatever we may think of the dangers of such learning (since it involves the control of one person, either consciously or unconsciously, by another), it is necessary. Human culture is partly the result of the fact that we do not have to learn everything all over again through trial and error. Thus, a child learns to avoid a hot stove by the repeated word "hot" in relation to the stove and either previous or current experiences of hotness. (This means that there is a certain amount of trial and error in the process, of course.)

Yet the fact that this process is automatic, continuous, and often unconscious points to its dangers. It means that the quality of life around a child is of utmost significance, since both "desirable" and "undesirable" reactions may be accepted by the child. Race prejudice, whatever its deeper origins, is probably actualized in the response-patterns of a child primarily through just such a process. Further, there is an alarming amount of evidence pointing toward our particular age as one which accepts fairly uncritically the responses which society in general and certain groups in particular demand.[5]

All of this indicates the ineffectiveness of an hour or two of Christian teaching on Sunday morning at the church unless the family takes seriously its teaching mission also and seeks to fulfill it on Christian terms. A previous generation which believed that the church could ignore adults and bring up a new generation of Christians conditioned to new responses has been proved sadly mistaken. The world does *not* move forward on the feet of little children; it rather is largely formed or *de*formed by adults who are responsible for the forming of younger selves before such selves have much of a chance for independent decision. For this reason the church is increasingly coming to see that its program of Christian education must be aimed fundamentally at parents and that any work it may do with children is relatively ineffective unless this is the case.

Thus, this approach to learning is not so much one that the church ought consciously to use (since it involves manipulation and thus the assumption of authority and power over one person by another), but rather it must recognize that conditioning *is* going on both in the church and outside it. Having recognized this to be the case, it must take it into account as it plans its program of nurture and teaching.

A *third* type of learning occurs primarily on the ideational level: namely, *rote learning* (or memorization of ideas). It is this approach that educational institutions, including the church, are continually tempted to depend upon. Further, when they do not emphasize it, they are often criticized for being too much concerned with "non-essentials." It may be that the reaction against the rote emphasis of the nineteenth century, both in general and in Christian education, has led to the placing of too little emphasis on learning the essential facts, ideas, and information which are part both of our general heritage

92

and our Christian heritage. Christian teaching must *impart* the basic understandings of the Christian faith, especially with respect to the Bible. A proper understanding of the heritage and some systematic arranging of its parts into a framework are essential. The pursuit of better intellectual understanding of the Christian faith is a worthy undertaking and must be taken more seriously by the Church than it now is, but this is not enough.

For an understanding of learning consonant with the view of the Church which has been presented, therefore, we must turn to a *fourth* view, namely that the most significant learning occurs through the experience we may call *personal and creative encounter.*[6] From a Christian point of view, nothing has really been learned until it affects one personally ("existentially") in terms of his relationships with the God and Father of our Lord Jesus Christ. Thus Christian learning involves, at least on its deeper levels, this personal encounter between the learner—in terms of his understanding and basic experience—and the Lord of Life.

Paul Tillich has stated this eloquently in his sermon, "What Is Truth?" With unusual insight and clarity, he denies that truth is finally contained in facts, reasoning, and scholarly statements, and asserts, instead, that learning must involve personal encounter. Those who are asked whether they have found in their studies a "truth which is relevant to their lives" are likely to agree "that it is not the scholarly work which can give truth relevant for our life." [7]

This is not to minimize scholarly pursuits (though some will take it as this), for such pursuits may point to the Truth. Even the teachings of and about Jesus as contained in the New Testament are not the Truth, though they point to it. The Truth is to be found in encounter, pointing beyond itself to God:

On this road you will meet the liberating truth in many forms except in one form: you never will meet it in the form of propositions which you can learn or write down and take home. But you may encounter it in one sentence of a book or of a conversation or of a lecture, or even of a sermon. This sentence is not the truth, but it may open you up for the truth and it may liberate you from the bondage of opinions and prejudices and conventions. Suddenly, true reality appears like the brightness of lightning in a formerly dark place. Or, slowly, true reality appears like a landscape when the fog becomes thinner and finally disappears. New darknesses, new fogs will fall upon you; but you have expereinced at least once, the truth and the freedom given by the truth. Or you may be grasped by the truth in an encounter with a piece of nature—its beauty and its transitoriness; or in an encounter with a human being in friendship and estrangement, in love, in difference and hate; or in an encounter with yourself in a sudden insight into the hidden strivings of your soul, in disgust and even hatred of yourself, in reconciliation with and acceptance of yourself. In these encounters you may meet the true reality—the truth which liberates from illusions and false authorities, from enslaving anxieties, desires and hostilities, from a wrong self-rejection and a wrong self-affirmation.[8]

As Tillich goes on to say, the Truth is found only as the human being is confronted by the ultimate Truth, the God revealed in Jesus Christ. This is what is meant when the Fourth Gospel records Jesus as saying, "I am the way, and the truth, and the life" (John 14:6, italics mine).

We meet and are met; there is imparted to us something which calls out from us a response; we are encountered by a person who becomes a means of truth for us. Often this meeting occurs only after long hours of intellectual pursuits, or of soul-searching, or even of despair, and thus it is related to the entire past history of the individual. There is much learning which precedes this deepest of all learning, and much Christian teaching must be in preparation for the encounter which we can only hope will occur. For although from the Christian perspective, this encounter becomes truly significant only as it includes the meeting of the human self with the divine Self, such a meeting is prepared for and mediated through the encounter with human selves. This means that Christian teaching occurs primarily in relationships, and only secondarily is it transmissive,[9] and both of these point beyond themselves to the encounter of the human self with the divine Self.

This insight has been admirably stated by Reuel Howe when he writes: "My faith is, therefore, that God uses my power of love, limited and sinful though it is, to prepare my child for the experience of His reconciling and fulfilling love." [10] To be sure, as he goes on to show, "Christian education is responsible for the continued recital of God's saving acts and of the transmission of the subject matter of the historical faith and life of the Christian community." [11] We cannot escape the obligation of making known (imparting) Christian truth, and this requires intellectual wrestling with as well as the acceptance of ideas by the learner.

The content of the Christian faith is the fruit of the action of the "Eternal Thou" in and through the "Thou" of Jesus of Nazareth in personal encounter with men. This encounter has content, and it can be identified, formulated, and interpreted. As such, however, it is only a part of the truth. Separated from the relationship out of which it came, it is without saving power. As unrelated content, it is in danger of becoming a substitute for the relationship, and therefore, an idol. We are not saved by knowledge alone, and yet without content a relationship can become formless, purposeless, and destructive. Only as my life is "hid with Christ in God" (Col. 3:3) can my knowing have its full meaning.[12]

This rather extended discourse on the deeper meaning of Christian nurture and teaching has been included because only as we come to see this are we likely to take seriously the entire teaching function of the Church. We cannot conclude that we have discharged our teaching responsibility when we have developed even a better-than-average church school. All that the Church can do directly and indirectly is demanded, since Christian nurture is that process by which a child, youth, or adult is brought into a creative relationship with God and established in that relationship.

Christian Education and All Ages

A third fact which must be taken into account is that *this nurture concerns those of all ages within the Christian community,* from birth to death, the infant in his mother's arms *and* the mature adult who has drunk either deeply or sparingly of the riches of life. It was to adults, not children, that the writer of Ephesians was speaking when he wrote: ". . . until we all attain to the unity of the faith and of the knowledge of the Son of God, to mature manhood, to the measure of the stature of the fullness of Christ . . . we are to grow up in every way into him who is the head, into Christ" (4:13, 15b).

Christian nurture must begin, then, even before the child is born, through the love and concern which the Church puts around the prospective parents. This will consist of pastoral and lay calls, and possibly of groups in which help can be given to couples expecting their first child.

Again, the responsibility of the Church during the first months of the child's life is primarily with the parents. A call immediately after birth by the pastor and one soon thereafter by the person designated to call on the mothers of new babies, sometimes called the nursery

95

home visitor, are vital. The latter will take the first step that deals directly with the child by enrolling him in the group which the church provides for children not yet old enough to attend sessions of the church school. The parents must be made to feel that even though their participation in church activities is greatly curtailed, they are still a part of the fellowship. Larger churches may be able to provide special groups geared to the schedules of the parents of young children.

For churches that practice infant baptism, this is the first corporate action of the Church on behalf of the child. As has already been pointed out, this is the act by which many churches accept the child, in the name of Christ, into their fellowship, not as a confirmed or believing member but still as a valid and significant member of the fellowship. For churches not practicing infant baptism, a dedication service is increasingly common. In either case, the Church, both the local congregation that performs the rite and any other church to which the child is taken by his parents, ought to be bound by the pledge of the Church to nurture the child in the Christian faith, just as the parents are made responsible by the fact of physical birth of the child into a Christian family. This is not meant to imply that the Church does not have an evangelistic mission to the unbaptized child; it does have a peculiar and undeniable obligation to the baptized or dedicated child.

Churches, both denominations and local groups, vary with regard to the age at which children are brought to the church building itself. Many now provide crib nurseries and "toddler" rooms for those under two years of age. Obviously all the church can do for such a child is to provide adequate care, though it is important that it take this task as seriously as it does its task of conscious teaching of older children. Sufficient space, competent care, facilities for warming bottles, appropriate toys, and means of safeguarding the health of such children must be provided. The selection of those who care for infants and toddlers should be made with as great regard to their welfare as is the selection of a teacher, let us say, for senior young people.[13]

What has been said about the care of those under two is equally pertinent for the two- and three-year-old groups. Indeed, not much more can be done for the two-year-old than is done for the toddler. Within recent years, however, some churches have provided guides for the leaders of this age.[14] Informal play in a happy, secure atmosphere lays the foundation on which later conscious teaching can occur.

With the three-year-old, some formal teaching can take place, though the emphasis still is on the atmosphere of the church-school group. It is of utmost importance that these children be treated as human beings, deserving of the respect that an adult demands. To be sure, the child must be dealt with in terms of his own capacities, and thus only rudimentary group life, the hearing of very brief stories, and the learning of such simple ethics as "taking turns" are possible.

At four years of age the child enters the church kindergarten. If possible there should be separate groups for the four- and five-year-olds, since there is considerable development from one age to the other. Even at four, however, the child is capable of increased social activities, of somewhat longer (but still very brief) stories, of brief moments of worship, and of simple group singing. At five the possibilities for such activities increase, and the reading of longer stories to the more developed children in a group is desirable if the space and leadership allow.

In all preschool groups the "atmosphere" is of utmost importance—that is, those things which unconsciously condition the child in his first contacts with the Church. Such things as the room itself, the equipment available, the freedom which is allowed, and especially the quality of the leadership present compose this atmosphere. There has been for several years a growing recognition that men ought to be included on the staffs of preschool groups, lest children unconsciously get the notion that the Church is for women and children. Also, boys tend to identify more readily with men teachers. An increasing number of churches (for example, Highland Park Methodist Church, Dallas, Texas, and First Methodist Church, Lubbock, Texas) have been successful in enlisting couples to work with preschool children.

What the Church does with the parents of preschool children is of equal, probably greater, importance than what it does for the children themselves. As we have indicated, it is somewhat absurd for the Church to expect to do much in an hour or two a week to offset what happens during the remaining hours of the child's life, since so much learning does occur through the unconscious conditioning of daily life. Some churches are successfully carrying out parent study groups, at the church-school hour or at some other time. Generally speaking, such groups will not be concerned so much with general problems of child-rearing as with such matters as the importance of providing love,

97

security, and discipline by parents;[15] ways of dealing with children's questions about God, nature, sex, and other topics (but not providing "pat" answers for parents to give to their children); the providing of books for the parents to use both for themselves and with the children; and the giving of other help as needed.

As a single example, in one church of medium size, First Methodist Church, Jacksonville, Texas, the Director of Christian Education organized a group of parents into a class meeting at the church-school hour on Sunday morning to discuss ways in which parents can deal with children's questions about such topics as Christ, prayer, death, and nature. Similar groups, meeting at other hours, have been introduced into many churches. Out of such groups there sometimes comes the realization on the part of parents that what they really need is a more adequate intellectual understanding of their own faith.

Other ways in which church and home can work together consist of regular parent-teacher meetings, visits by teachers or associate teachers in the home, and the provision of books and magazines. The magazine for parents published by the denomination involved (for example, *The Christian Home*, provided by the Methodist Church [16]) is sometimes sent or taken to all new parents.

It is not alone the *church school* that is responsible for even the preschool child: the *entire church family* must seek to welcome and nurture the children who belong to that family. The pastor will think of himself as pastor of the children as well as youth and adults. By visits to church-school groups and in the home, he will become a familiar and loved friend of the children of his congregation. One pastor, for example, makes a point of being able to call the names of all children when he visits in any home.

After the child enters school, the ideational content of the church-school program should be increased. This is not the place to discuss the amount of Bible knowledge that ought to be taught to each age group. Suffice it to say that the present position maintained by any denomination ought not to be thought of as a final one, since this is a question which is currently being rethought. It would appear that if we have erred within recent years, it has been in the direction of not teaching enough such content. Yet it must be remembered that the Bible is an adult book, and the child must be introduced to it in such a manner that he will not be repelled by it but rather come to see it as something which has significance for his own life.

98

This will mean that the child ought to be guided into an understanding of the Bible sufficient to provide a substantial undergirding for the more mature learning which can take place during the adolescent period. The same thing must be remembered with regard to the other "content" areas of the Christian faith: the faith (theology) of the Church, the meaning of the Good News, the history of the Christian community, the meaning of worship, the meaning of symbols, current expressions of faith in committed individuals. Indeed, this same assertion can be made about the child's own relationship with God. He should not be pushed too far, for he is an immature person; yet he must continually be led beyond his present knowledge and understanding, step by step,[17] with the hope that by the time he reaches adolescence he will have the basis on which a mature faith can begin to be built. The vacation church school, weekday sessions, summer camps, and a wide variety of educational activities can help to further this process.

Over and beyond his participation in the Sunday and weekday church school, the elementary school child should be made to feel a real part of the larger Church fellowship. Children's choirs are a means of doing this, especially when they participate in the morning service or at other times not with the idea of "showing off" but rather with the understanding that they are participating in a service of worship. Family activities at the church should include children not in a perfunctory manner (that is, just allowing them to attend), but rather in a manner which involves them in participation (through such activities as singing, playing games, reading responsively, and the like). "Family nights" are one way in which this concern is implemented, such programs consisting of at least one period when the family joins together for eating, recreation, or worship.

The matter of the participation by children in the service of worship was discussed briefly in a previous chapter. Practices will vary concerning this, though there would appear to be little argument against those of junior age and above so participating, and there are many reasons why children of even a younger age ought to participate at least occasionally and perhaps regularly. The emphasis in the new curriculum of the Protestant Episcopal Church on an early family worship service preceding the church-school hour points toward a helpful addition in this regard.

The act of confirmation (or joining the Church through a voluntary act), which perhaps ought to be postponed to the junior-high level, should be made especially significant. Membership classes are increasingly common even in the non-confessional communions, and it is well that they are. Probably the church-school emphasis for six months prior to the assuming of the vows of the covenant could be given to such preparation. If this is not done then a minimum of a dozen sessions should be held. Further, the service when the boy or girl accepts for himself the covenantal relationship with Christ ought to be made sufficiently meaningful that it will be remembered throughout life. To put it another way, the membership service should be conducted in such a manner that it is potentially a real service of worship and commitment.[18]

The junior-high age (grades 7, 8, 9) is a difficult one with which to deal, since it is the time when puberty begins for most boys and girls. Added to other problems is the fact that girls mature ordinarily a year earlier than boys, so that the group consists of both children and adolescents. As a partial solution to the problem, many churches have adopted the three-department rather than the two-department youth division, with seventh and eighth graders together, ninth and tenth, and eleventh and twelfth.

Neither children nor youth, this group proves baffling to many church leaders; and partly as a consequence of the ensuing lack of understanding and neglect, together with fewer restraints placed upon them by the family, they often begin to drift away from the Church. There are many *ideas* that should be taught at this age, and reasonable efforts can be made to improve the intellectual content of the church's program of nurture. But of greater significance is the broader concept of nurture which we have been discussing, the ministering to the immediate needs of these early teen-agers to have a sense of belonging, to experience acceptance, and to be given increasing opportunities for independent expression. Not every adult ought to be asked to work with this age: only those who can respect the early teen-ager as a person in spite of his uncertain status in life are likely to be helpful.

Although senior-high young people are ready for a greater emphasis on the meaning of the Christian faith, they too must be given as much freedom as possible in the planning of their program. Quite often, however, we underestimate the deep questions and longings of ado-

100

lescence and try to "hold them to the church" by a program of recreation. This almost invariably fails. It is at this age that the Youth Fellowship as a self-conscious group can come into full flower. Opportunities for leadership development must be offered, and a chance to develop a more mature understanding of the meaning of life in the perspective of the Christian faith should be made available. Through increased responsibilities in the church, senior-high young people come to feel a growing participation in the larger fellowship. All youth groups need the special help which can come through participation in Youth Activities Week, summer camps and assemblies, week-end retreats and work camps, and other short-term agencies.

One other factor needs special mention: namely, it is at adolescence that genuine commitment and decision on a deeper level than previously possible can take place. One need not repeat the excess of the psychology of G. Stanley Hall and Edwin Starbuck at the turn of the century in order to make this assertion, for adolescence is a time of rapid change and readjustment any way you look at it in our diverse culture. Even though children are taken into full church membership prior to this period, it should not be assumed that they have entered fully and freely into the covenant relationship. Hence ample opportunities for public response to God's claim in Christ should be given both in the local fellowship and at summer camps and assemblies. Further, young people at the senior age should be given opportunity (but in no way coerced) for responding vocationally in terms of full-time church work.

The need for Christian nurture does not end with graduation from high school. Those who do not attend college are normally thrust into adult responsibilities and from henceforth must be treated as adults. Work with college young people is too specialized to receive even brief mention here, though its unusual importance should be pointed out. Whether the person is in college or is working, this age is a time when life is broadening, horizons are expanding, and serious doubts about the meaning and purpose of life may arise. Thus, it is especially important that the ideational content of teaching be emphasized, and that both a mature consideration of the meaning of the Christian faith and of the meaning of life in the light of that faith ought to be provided.

Adults too need opportunities for maturing in the Christian faith. The Sunday school class offers some opportunities for study, even more for fellowship, but is badly in need of reformation, since so many have become either little "churches" or social clubs. Thus the program of adult education must go much beyond the Sunday-school class and include Bible-study groups, parents' groups, groups of persons meeting together to discuss the relevance of the Christian faith to their occupations, and the like. These will be discussed at greater length in the following chapter.

A new area of concern for the Church consists of those who have reached mature years—usually sixty to sixty-five and up. At these ages the primary need is often for groups formed to provide association with those of a similar age. "Golden Age" clubs and similar activities are increasing in number and popularity.[19] The pastoral ministry to this group, especially those who are unable to attend church meetings, is also of prime importance.

A Family-centered Emphasis

The emphasis which we have just made on the separation of persons in terms of their ages with their accompanying needs and capacities should not be taken as the entire picture. Although we shall surely not want to lose the emphasis on *graded* activities, we have come to realize within recent years that this aspect of our programs of Christian nurture has been taken too far. The church has, along with numerous other forces, helped to tear the family apart. We have at a number of places already mentioned the necessity of family-centered activities: worship, recreation, fellowship. Therefore, as a fourth emphasis, we may say that *the Church's concern for Christian nurture must include an interest in the family as a unit.* This will mean not alone the effort to help parents, or to effect home-church co-operation, but also an attempt to bring the family *as a family* into various church activities.

Obviously what has been written in this section and in previous ones is not intended to be a complete description of the continuing nurture which the Church ought to give at all age levels and to the family as a unit. Rather, it is offered only as illustrative of this responsibility. Only such a broad program is likely to provide the opportunities in which creative encounter may take place. Or to put it another way, our modern facilities together with our understanding of the human person and how he learns place upon us the responsibility for creating situations in ways previously unheard and undreamed of, situations in which it may be that the Holy Spirit can work to effect commitment, maturity, and unity.

The Curriculum of Learning

A fifth emphasis that can be made only briefly concerns the content (or curriculum) of Christian nurture. We have repeatedly said that verbalizations *about* the Christian faith are not enough; participation in Christian community is essential. As Reuel Howe has pointed out, the Church has depended too much on words, not enough on relationships.[20] If what we have asserted concerning the Church—namely, that its essential quality is *koinonia*, that it must be a *redemptive fellowship*—is true, then the theological basis for this point of view seems sound. From this perspective, then, the content of learning is the total meaning of all that happens: words, relationships, deeds, action, participation. The curriculum is, in the final analysis, what the person takes home with him.[21]

Nevertheless, as we have also insisted, this is not to minimize the place of bodies of material in the teaching process. The Bible especially will be the source of such material—the Bible as the record of God's search for man, of man's response to God both in faith and in unfaith. As the Bible is made clear to the learner as the record of God's self-revelation to man, culminating in him who *is* the way, the truth, and the life, it will take on new meaning and significance. Especially as it is shown to deal with the deeper issues and problems of life it will become more than a book of ancient vintage to be revered but not to be taken in all seriousness. Only in this way can the Bible become the vehicle for God's revelation to us today.

At every possible point in the program of teaching and nurture, the material in the Bible, its background, its original meaning, and its meaning for us today will be communicated. Further, other bodies of material—the history of the Christian community, theologizing based on the biblical revelation, the story of the Christian enterprise today—will be made known to children, youth, and adults. It must be recognized, however, that this is likely to be less than redemptive in nature unless it is communicated within a community which is redemptive, where there are love, acceptance, and forgiveness.

The heart of the content, then, will be creative encounter—between man and man and between man and God. This takes place in community. The Church must, at least to some extent, be a fellowship of love and concern before it can communicate the *message* of love and concern. Human reconciliation points to divine reconciliation, human love to divine love. Surely it is God's love for us that makes it possible for us to love (I John 4:19); it is God's reconciliation (acceptance) that makes our acceptance of others possible (II Cor. 5:18-19); it is God's creation of a new being within us that makes us ambassadors of this Good News to others (II Cor. 5:17-20). The initiative is always God's but our response to God's self-giving love not only makes possible but also makes necessary our efforts to communicate this love to others.

What, Then, Is Christian Education?

This leads us to a final consideration which is a kind of summary of what has gone before: namely, *the nature and function of the educational office of the Church.* We have ruled out either directly or indirectly several widely accepted views. For example, it is not alone to impart knowledge *about* the Christian faith, or even the contents *of* the Bible, as the nineteenth-century Sunday school tended to do. To be sure, it *is* concerned with such impartation, and we are now rediscovering the importance of the biblical and theological foundations for Christian teachings.[22] But Christian nurture is concerned with *more* than this.

Again, the purpose of Christian education is not primarily to bring about character formation, such as progressive religious education tended to insist and such as is characteristic still of much of our material in Christian education.[23] The ethical implications of the gospel are important, of course, and one of the aspects of Christian teaching is to help persons become aware of these meanings, but it is more than this also.

Nor is the purpose of Christian education solely to lead to conversion or confirmation, though it is vitally concerned with decision and commitment, and with affiliation with and education into the organized church. Christian nurture involves all of these but cannot be contained in any of these or in other particularistic interpretations.

What, then, is the nature and function of Christian nurture and teaching? To attempt a definition is to risk being presumptuous, yet such must be done. The purpose of Christian education, briefly stated, is to seek to lead persons into a living encounter with the God and Father of our Lord Jesus Christ, and to illuminate and enlighten the meaning of this encounter for all of life. The means through which this takes place are dynamic encounters with other persons whose lives have been touched by Jesus Christ, and whose spirit, attitudes, knowledge, and understanding have in some measure been formed and informed by him. The role of the leader is to be a human channel by which the Spirit of God may reach others. He performs this role partly through introducing those whom he teaches to the knowledge of the Christian faith. As Lewis Sherrill has put it:

> It may be said, then, that *the means to the ends sought* in Christian education are such as: introducing persons to the Christian community, introducing them to the Bible and the Christian heritage, preparing the way for personal response to revelation, participating with them in purposeful action, and counseling with them during periods of crisis.[24]

This means, then, that there is no real dichotomy between nurture and evangelism, no absolute division between *kērygma* and *didachē*, no neat packaging of the offices of the Christian community. The human self is a unity; so must be the Body of Christ. Yet there is a distinctive function of Christian teaching when it is thought of in the narrow sense of that which is planned to take place in the church-school class or in some other educational enterprise: namely, to prepare for and follow up after the distinctive meetings of the human self with the divine Self. Such meetings cannot, in the final analysis, be either planned or structured. Preparation for them can be made, however. Such encounters may take place at summer camps and conferences, in the church-school classroom, in church worship services, at evangelistic services, in private meditation, sometimes when least expected. When they do occur, it may be reasonably inferred that the efforts of parents or substitute parents, of church-school teachers and other church leaders, of pastors and counselors, of friends and associates, have helped prepare the way for that person's encounter with the living God. It may be a dying Stephen for Paul, a mother's concern for Augustine, a Peter Bohler for John Wesley, a concerned church-school teacher for John Smith.

Further, it is certain that there will be need for follow-up and nurture after such encounters, as the person, be he child, youth, or adult, seeks to understand the implications of commitment and to live by it. Paul sought out Ananias and spent many years before beginning his mission to the Gentiles. With many there is no dramatic encounter like Paul's, and there is need for many encounters, much preparation, much follow-up.

As Paul later wrote: "I planted, Apollos watered, but God gave the growth" (I Cor. 3:6). The planting and the watering are the human task; the growth is the divine gift. Christian nurture takes place within the Christian community. It in turn helps to plant the seeds, to till the soil, for the inception of true community. The Church must teach to be the Church. Indeed, as it teaches it becomes more truly the Church. In the fellowship of searching, of learning, of seeking together, and of responding corporately to God's initiative, true *koinonia* may emerge.

VIII

Group Life Within the Fellowship

REPEATEDLY THROUGHOUT THIS DISCUSSION, AND PARTICULARLY IN the preceding chapter, much has been said concerning the existence of smaller groups within the larger Church. One of the by-products of the Sunday-school movement has been that it has provided a framework in which children, youth, and adults have found face-to-face relationships with one another and with more mature leaders. There have been, and still are, other types of smaller groups. One of the finest examples in the history of the Christian movement was the class meeting for which John Wesley was responsible and which continued to be a vital part of the Methodist movement for some decades after his time. Such a group, consisting of approximately twelve persons, met together to discuss common and individual problems, confess their sins to one another, and otherwise help each other in the Christian life.

Since the process of nurturing life, whether it be physical, mental, or spiritual, takes place within concrete situations involving persons, such small groups, of which the family has been and still is the prime example, are absolutely essential. Further, such small groups within the church appear to be one means by which the *koinonia* of which we have spoken so often may be encouraged.

Mass Media or Face-to-Face Groups?

It may appear that with modern means of mass communication, and with the development of a kind of "mass mind," the importance of face-to-face groups is diminishing. Certainly, for good or ill, much of the teaching and nurture which take place in twentieth-century America occurs through popular reading material, motion pictures, radio-television, and similar means of mass communication. Both individual and group behavior are no doubt increasingly controlled by these cultural forces which originate outside the immediate milieu of any small group such as the family, play group, social club, school, or religious organization. Fashions are set by Paris or Hollywood; popular music tastes are controlled by disc jockeys; teen-age habits are influenced by motion picture and television script-writers.

Indeed, David Riesman has a weight of evidence to support his contention that we are entering (perhaps have already entered) an "other-directed" culture in which independent thinking is largely submerged. "What is common to all the other-directed people," he writes, "is that their contemporaries are the source of direction for the individual—either those known to him or those with whom he is indirectly acquainted, through friends and through the mass media." [1] The high-school gang may be the immediate source of direction to its members, but the high-school gang itself is likely to receive its direction from sources outside itself.

In the face of such cultural forces, the Church must also seek to use effectively the mass media for communicating the gospel. Nor are the traditional means, such as mass evangelism, adequate to offset the influence of the non-Christian and sub-Christian use of modern media. The Church has been far too negligent in utilizing radio and television for making known the Gospel to the masses. There does not appear to be any likelihood, however, that the organized Church is going to be able to compete with the other forces that make use of such means as the motion picture, television, and advertizing for commercial and entertainment purposes. We must do all we can, but it may be that we shall have to aim our major efforts at the disciplined minority rather than toward the captured millions.

Indeed, historically the Church has never been content in using mass means for spreading the gospel. The examples in the New Testament which record preaching to large groups, such as that at Pentecost, are offset by those in which the person-to-person approach was made.[2] John Wesley and his associates were as successful as any group has ever been in the use of mass evangelism, yet Wesley was careful to organize his converts into societies and class meetings. A report on Billy Graham, who has used mass evangelism more fully than any other modern preacher, records that he conceded in a meeting with British churchmen in 1955 that mass evangelism is one of the least effective methods of winning persons to Christ. "How much more effective," he is reported as having said, "it would be if Christian laity themselves proclaimed the gospel to other men and women!" [3] Further, his use of smaller groups in connection with mass revivals is illustrative of his recognition of the need for small groups as well as mass meetings. Indeed, the character of the Christian gospel itself, demanding as it does decision in freedom, is such that face-to-face communication is needed.

Actually there is no point in arguing the superior virtues of these two approaches to communicating the gospel. Both must be used to serve different needs: mass means to acquaint people with the existence and general nature of the gospel and the demands which it places upon us, the small group to effect intelligent and free decision made in community but yet in freedom. It may be affirmed, however, that in a day when public opinion is so largely formed by the mass media, and when personal identity tends to be lost in a crowd culture, it is even more important than before for the Church to seek every opportunity available to provide small groups in which personal identity can be recovered and responsible decision be effected.

The Importance of the Small Group

The fact is that most Christian nurture does take place within smaller groups. The uplifting of moral standards, the awakening of the masses, and the general witness of the Church no doubt do occur as the result of a sermon preached effectively to 75,000 in a football stadium, or as the result of an effective dramatic program beamed to a television audience of several million. The long process of encouraging Christian maturity is, and is likely to remain, a function of the small group or the person-to-person ministry.

This face-to-face type of association is, of course, not the concern of the Church alone. Many community agencies provide such groups. Agencies other than the Church, for example, are concerned that the family will be aided in performing its role more adequately than it now is. Current thinking concerning juvenile delinquency almost invariably indicates that the breakdown of the family as an effective group is one of the causes, if not the primary cause, of such behavior. In this knowledge and with the conviction that something must be done, those engaged in the field of group work and the newer offspring, group dynamics, have been working in an effort to understand more fully the nature and function of group life, as well as seeking means of providing group experiences for those who are lost in the lonely crowd.

This knowledge, like all "wisdom of the world," may be used by the Church to further its purposes. There is always the danger, of course, that in adopting the techniques of the "secular" community, it will also adopt its basic orientation. We must be vigilant, for example, lest we come to think that by the ultization of our knowledge of the dynamics of group structure and functioning we have formed a group in which the Spirit of God can work: perhaps we have, perhaps not. But, we are remiss unless we utilize this knowledge in the hope that through what we do Christian unity and *koinonia* may come into being.

The Nature of a Group

Let us now briefly summarize some of the knowledge concerning group life which can be of help to us. The *first* question we must face concerns *the nature of a group.*

S. R. Slavson has aptly defined a group "as consisting of three or more persons in an informal relation where there is a maximum interpenetration and prolonged direct emotional activity among the individuals constituting it, and as a result of which the personality of each member is modified." [4] It may be possible for a larger aggregation of people to become a group—that is, more than fifteen or twenty—and indeed in the Christian community it is our hope that in one sense the entire congregation will be this. Yet the very fact that interpenetration and interstimulation become physically and spatially difficult when there are more than twelve to fifteen members argues for the small group (at least under twenty members) for youth, adults, and children.

Paul Maves has set forth the following characteristics of a group:

1. There is *direct* and *frequent interaction.* . . .
2. It has *a common task, problem, purpose,* or *center* which gives it cohesiveness and unity although it may meet a variety of needs. . . .
3. It has *a mechanism for arriving at decisions* so that at least a minimum of organization or structure is necessary.
4. It has *leadership* or a division of responsibilities which enables it to integrate its activities and carry out its functions successfully.
5. It has an *atmosphere* and a *basic imagery* of its own which give it a sense of differentiation or a "we" feeling. This may be symbolized by insignia, names, dress, ritual actions, or written codes. . . .
6. It has *a way of selecting its membership* so the group can control and be responsible for its own conduct.[5]

A nonchurch group, then, consists of a self-conscious unit of individuals, who, in some measure, submit their own individuality to the group. Its purposes include an attempt to modify behavior, to change attitudes and habits, and to be a socializing influence. It may have a more specific purpose, like the imparting of skills or information, in which case the group may be defined as "task centered." When no such specific purpose is involved, it may be called "need centered." [6]

To put it more concretely, some groups are "task-centered" because they exist primarily to get a job done—to learn a body of material, to build a fence, to clean the church lawn. Actually an aggregate of people who perform such a task may or may not be a group according to the definition above. In fact, the task assigned to a group may not be the real reason why a collection of individuals becomes a group. This is especially true with respect to church groups, most of which are task centered, even though they may hold together because they satisfy individual and group needs which are different from the task assigned it. For example, a youth group may be a real group not because of the body of material which the church feels it ought to assimilate but because of the need which the members have for social fulfillment. Many adult Sunday-school classes are only remotely interested in "learning about the Bible," but are quite anxious to enjoy group association. In such cases the local church and its leaders face the problem as to how much attempt can be made to structure the task for which the group was created. This same problem, of course, may exist for other agencies.[7]

Church groups obviously are similar to nonchurch groups, though the problem for the Church is not simply one of bringing a group into being. If this is all that happens, then the person involved might just as well be participating in a social or community agency which has high moral standards. The ultimate purpose of all Church groups, regardless of what the immediate purpose may be, must be conceived of, in some measure, as an attempt to effect encounter with the living God, or to follow up from that encounter in study, fellowship, and action.

For example, the finance committee, whose immediate purpose is to provide for the financial needs of the local church and its outreach, ceases to be a *Church* group when it fails to see its work as, in a real sense, implementing the concern of the members and the entire congregation for the Christian cause. The assimilating of bodies of material by a church-school class, while a legitimate assigned task, may become a secular rather than a religious act unless through study together a sense of Christian community emerges. Church groups, while

111

subject to the same dynamics as all other groups, must be units in which *koinonia* develops if they are truly Christian.

The Nature of Leadership

The study of group life has also involved considerable attention to *the nature of leadership,* our *second* matter for discussion. There are two major types of leaders: first, the "natural" leader, or that which emerges out of the group in the form of an elected chairman or as someone who simply "takes charge" because he can secure a following. Second, there is the "forced" leader, that which an agency provides for a group. This may be a club leader, a counselor for a church youth group, a church-school teacher, the pastor of the church (who, though chosen by many congregations, does not usually emerge out of the congregation). Leaders of children's groups are almost always "forced" leaders; youth groups possess both kinds; while adult groups often choose their leadership. What is said in the following paragraphs may be applied to both types of leaders.

What about the nature and amount of leadership which a leader can and ought to assume? Leadership implies a particular responsibility assumed by one person for dealing with other individuals. It is assumed that the leader has a greater responsibility for guiding the destiny of the group than other members but not necessarily a determinative function. Indeed, in the Protestant movement when the priesthood of the laity is taken seriously, there can hardly be a conception of leadership which conceives the leader's role as domination. The nature of the Christian faith, with its emphasis on responsible decision, seems to point in the direction of a leader who works *with* people while giving positive leadership rather than one who *dominates.* Leadership inevitably involves guidance and the responsibility in some situations to make independent decisions, but it does not necessarily imply the use of the kind of authority which involves dictatorship.

Help in understanding the dynamics of group leadership may also be secured by turning to experiments which have been conducted by social psychologists. The most famous of these involved a study of three types of leaders, the autocratic, the *laissez faire,* and the democratic. In this study, begun by Ronald Lippitt, with the later help of Kurt Lewin and Ralph K. White,[8] a deliberate attempt was made to check the results of these three types of leadership in boys' clubs, with specified clubs being provided in rotation with the three types of leaders. The authoritarian leader completely determined policy, techniques, methods of work, and step-by-step procedures. The *laissez-faire* leader really gave no leadership, did not participate in the activities, and was there mostly as an observer, available to answer questions when they were asked. The democratic leader participated actively in the group, but the group itself decided on policy, planned a method of work, and carried out the plans.[9] The leader gave technical advice and helped throughout the process as needed. In Biblical terms, he was servant, not master, of the group. (See John 13:12-17 and Luke 22:27.)

The observable results of the experiment offer no conclusive proof of anything, but they do point to several principles with respect to the most effective use of leadership.

1. The absence of active leadership (the so-called *laissez-faire* approach) leads to chaos and a lack of accomplishment.

2. Autocratic leadership (where the leader imposes his will on the group) brings about task-results, but it leads either to apathy on the part of members, or to aggressive behavior. In other words, some give up and do the will of the leader; others do as little as they can get by with and take out their aggression on other members, the leader, or someone outside the group.[10]

3. Democratic leadership is not a "soft democracy" or a modified "let alone" policy, but something different from both. The leader is active and thus provides a positive force in the decisions and deliberations of the group without dominating. Behavior of groups under such leadership tends to change from "hostility to friendliness, from egocentricism to we-feeling and to an objective, matter-of-fact attitude."[11]

To put this in theological language, the group under democratic leadership is more likely to be one in which a person can be himself, have the experience of group acceptance, be sufficiently free to be confronted by the living God, and grow toward Christian maturity. Instrumentally, it may be said that such leadership in the local church produces responsible churchmanship. The autocratic church leader is quite likely to "get the job done," but members of the church have little opportunity for maturing either in their ability to accept freedom or to assume responsible leadership. This is not to imply that there is no need for the individualist: the thundering Amos who speaks to a hostile Israel, the prophet who may be without honor in his own congregation. Such persons may awaken a congregation or a smaller group, but there is need for the leader who follows such an Amos to guide individuals into constructive means of expressing the prophet's message.

The nature and amount of leadership required by particular groups will naturally vary. The following principles for determining the amount of leadership to be given are only suggestive.

1. *The age of the group members.* In general, the older the members of the group, the less outside leadership is necessary and the more responsibility members of the group can assume. Young children need a maximum amount of adult leadership; junior-high young people must have leadership by adults but be given an increasing amount of freedom; senior young people should be given as much freedom as they are able to use.

2. *The past experience of the group.* If a group of seniors has had no experience in the group process, they will fail badly when suddenly given freedom. The wise group leader learns how much freedom a group can use immediately, and moves in the direction of granting freedom as responsibility is accepted.

3. *The amount of freedom which the agency (or church) allows.* For example, it may be a good thing for a teacher of junior high boys and girls to "forget about the lesson" and concentrate on the building of good interpersonal relations; yet some churches will not allow such freedom. The group leader must know the limitations which are placed on the group by the nature of the parent organization. Then one of his tasks becomes that of interpreting to the group the limitations to their freedom.

4. *The personality and past experience of the leader.* Leaders are persons, too, and they cannot be who they are not. Some leaders find it extremely difficult to avoid being autocratic. Such persons should be placed in position of leadership, if they must be used at all, where such an attitude is least harmful.

5. *Facilities, equipment, and space.* A teacher in a one-room church can give less freedom, especially of movement, than a teacher who has a separate room. Such practical matters must be taken into account.

Whatever limitations must be placed on the granting of freedom for the time being ought to be thought of as temporary, however. The goal of a democratic group is the development of the free, responsible citizen. The goal of the Church group is the maturing of the free, responsible Christian, standing, finally, before no man, but only God.

The Church Group

As we have discussed various matters concerning the nature of the group and of leadership, we have tried to show their relationship to church groups. Let us now look at some of the broader implications for the Church.[12]

1. For one thing, every person in a local church ought to be a member of at least one small group. What these groups are, along with possible new ones, will be discussed shortly.

2. Wherever possible, existing groups, most of which are task-centered, should be modified so that they may also be need-centered. These needs will be conceived of not only in the more superficial sense ("felt needs"), but also in the deeper sense ("existential needs"). This may mean, for example, that the nature of the teaching task will be thought of less as passing on a body of material and more as dealing with the deeper issues of life in the light of the biblical faith. Part of the teaching process is the re-evaluation of needs so that superficial "wants" are transformed into "existential needs."

3. New groups should be developed which are distinctly need-centered. The starting point may be what was previously described as "felt needs." For example, a group of single young adults in an urban church may feel the need for a Sunday dinner group to avoid having Sunday dinner alone. A group of parents may have as the starting point for a study group how to deal with the questions which children ask. A Bible-study group may have as its beginning point a desire not to be biblically illiterate. It is the responsibility of the leader in such instances to take the group where it is and seek to lead it into a recognition of its deeper needs: for example, the need to take seriously the biblical *message*.

4. A maximum amount of freedom and flexibility should be allowed within the limits fixed by denominational and local church policies. For example, many churches are fairly strict on the use of denominational church-school materials. Usually, however, the education committee of the church will give approval for the use of other materials if they are carefully chosen and not out of harmony with denominational principles. Youth groups may be encouraged to plan their own Sunday-evening-fellowship programs, and an adult church-school class may be allowed to follow an elective system of choosing class topics.

5. An attempt should be made to keep these groups small enough to

115

serve the needs of the members. As Maves puts it, "The size of groups will be determined not by publicity values but by the function to be served." [13]

6. Help should be given to the leaders of groups to the end that they will encourage the widest possible participation by members. This should include the chairmen of committees and other administrative groups. Further suggestions in this regard will be made subsequently.

In summary it should be said that those responsible for the over-all program of the local church should encourage the widest possible participation by church members in small groups, and should in turn give the kind of guidance to the leaders of these groups so that membership will be a dynamic and freeing experience.

Types of Existing Church Groups

Let us look now at the groups already in existence in most local churches. Sunday-school classes, weekday classes, Sunday-evening study groups—these and various other study groups whose distinctive purpose is educational are potentially groups in the sense that they have been described in this chapter. True, many such classes are too large, and it may not be worth the effort to break them into smaller ones. Some large classes partially solve this problem through the organization of subgroups for fellowship and recreation. The introduction of "buzz groups" into the actual class session (that is, smaller groups which discuss for five minutes or so a question presented by the teacher) may help.[14]

Where possible small classes ought to be organized. In one church a group of young couples were dissatisfied with any existing Sunday-school class and began meeting, with the approval of the church, to do their own Bible study. Later a competent leader was found, but the class continued to use such Bible helps as *The Abingdon Bible Commentary* and similar books. Reports were regularly made by class members, and the group carried out its name, "The Couples' Round Table," by literally meeting around a table. In another church an associate pastor was responsible for organizing a new forum group which became so interested in the various religious groups of the community that representatives from some of these groups were asked to meet with the class to present their own views. Through such an experience the members of the group came to a better understanding of their own faith.

Still another church-school class has been meeting together for more than eight years, choosing its own course of study by means of interest-finders and refusing to become too large for its entire membership to meet in the homes of the members. In order to assure this, the class has refused to accept, when offered, a larger meeting place, allowing another class with a desire to grow larger to have the more commodious room instead. New members are added as old ones move away, but the size of the group remains essentially the same.

The administrative agencies of the local fellowship are also potentially real groups, though many are not now so constituted and in many instances only a change in leadership would make this possible. To fail to point them in the direction of creative group life is to miss an opportunity for improving the total life of the parish, however.[15]

The various church organizations—women's society, men's club, youth fellowship, and the like—are also potentially more effective as groups. In many instances it is primarily a matter of training leadership so that they are able to accept the responsibilities of such creative group participation.

Departmental meetings of teachers also offer an opportunity for deeper group life, provided the meetings consist of more than the handling of emergencies. If teachers, especially of children and youth, could be helped to see the significance of their task, to achieve a more adequate understanding of its nature, and to face honestly and seriously the problems and needs of the members of their groups, then a fellowship might emerge which would lead to Christian *koinonia*. In one church a "Teaching Fellowship" was organized consisting only of teachers in the church school, to meet regularly in order to come to appreciate more fully the significance of the teaching task in the Church.

In all of these and in other existing aggregates of persons in the church, a deeper understanding of Christian *koinonia* is essential. Unless there is commitment to the Christ who stands behind, in judgment over, but in love for, all organizations, committees, and classes, the quality of fellowship will probably be no better than that which exists in nonchurch groups, perhaps not so good. An emphasis upon love, acceptance, and forgiveness should be made, and the claims of the gospel should be made clear. None of these emphases will guarantee either a response from the members or the development of *koinonia*. We can only have faith that our efforts may help it to come into being.

The Formation of New Groups

Further, because existing groups may be unwilling to change,[16] and because they do not fulfill all the existing or potential needs of a congregation, it will be well to encourage the inception of new groups, many of which may be formed on the basis of needs rather than tasks. Succeeding paragraphs only suggest examples of what may be done.

On the local church level, they may take a variety of forms: for example, they may be Bible-study groups meeting either in the home or at the church, or discussion groups centered around a variety of subjects. The best known of such efforts to effect "lay theological education" is the plan carried out by Robert E. Chiles in the Methodist Church of Concord, Ohio. In his own words:

Different classes are offered during each of three quarters of the regular school year. Each class meets for ten Tuesday evenings from eight until about ten o'clock. A four-year cycle of courses has been set up divided among historical, biblical, and theological studies. The registration fee ($5.00) includes the textbook and incidental expenses, and adds to the fund for the purchase of additional books for the church library.[17]

Receiving their inspiration from this experiment, several recent theology graduates have set up similar classes in their churches—one in California, another in Indiana, still another in Maryland.

A similar experiment has been described as occurring in a church in Denver, Colorado:

As one minister out of four in a congregation of over 3,800 people, I have had an unusual opportunity in helping to develop a network of study groups throughout the church. It is avowedly a ministry to a minority. The groups are small, varying in size from five to sixteen people. There is no one rigid pattern of makeup of these study groups. Some are made up of housewives, who meet in the morning twice a month; others . . . meet in a downtown hotel for their lunch and study. . . .

The intent in forming these groups is made quite clear from the start. They are small communities for learning. The focus of study varies from recent Broadway plays to current theological texts.[18]

The purpose of these groups is threefold: to give opportunity for people to "extend and renew their education"; "to help the layman express his religious questions"; and "to restore the ministry of the laity." [19]

Less formal groups are also existent in some churches. On the youth level these need-centered groups are sometimes called "cell" groups, though because of the communist use of the word it may not be a good term.[20] One church, for example, with only a little encouragement from staff members, formed a special group of its "volunteers" for full-time church work, this group holding occasional meetings. In another church a group of young couples, led by an officer in the Air Force, began meeting for Bible study without any formal organization. Prayer groups are perhaps the most common of such groups for adults. The purpose in these instances is always focused on meeting some need—either that of the members or of persons outside—instead of on a particular task.

A British clergyman describes the emergence of such a group in his parish in the following words:

Within my own congregation there began to emerge, after the first Mission of Visitation, a small and inarticulate group of people who were really concerned to explore at the deepest level the meaning of their membership in the Church. As time passed I began to realize that here in this group there was the nucleus of a dynamic community, a "Church within a Church," which bore at least some trace of that first *koinonia* which challenged the pagan world and planted the Cross at the heart of the Roman Empire. . . .

As the congregational group began to discover its existence, so it began also to discover its function. First of all, the group exists as a training school in Christian discipleship. . . . The group has a second function which can only be described as "an attempt to restore the parochial community." . . . the third function of the group is the outcome of the first two. It exists as an evangelizing agency—or more correctly, it provides an outlet in which its members can find the opportunity to express their faith in terms of service.[21]

A few churches have experimented with the formation of groups directly aimed at psychotherapy. Such groups require trained leadership, however, both for the leadership of the group and for the personal counseling which emerges out of the group. There would seem to be no reason, however, why some group similar to the Methodist class meeting could not be more widely used.

Another approach is the establishing of neighborhood groups. This is especially helpful in urban areas where the parish boundaries are apt to be quite wide, though there is one report of a rural parish that inaugurated this plan. Under such an arrangement, a neighborhood leader and one or more assistants are responsible for periodic visitation of the members in his area and for occasional group meetings. The type of discussion at such meetings will obviously vary greatly, and in many instances it never goes beyond the social level. Several churches have organized such neighborhood meetings around either a radio or television program sponsored by the church. In some instances such neighborhood groups have become permanent, one such group carrying out various projects of social service, and holding regular meetings.

The parish week end, so called by the Episcopal Church, likewise offers possibility for deepened fellowship. Either the entire church or the leaders in a larger one spend all or part of a week end, not so much in planning the work of the church as in discussing the deeper implications of what is being done.[22] Although this plan is especially encouraged by the Protestant Episcopal Church, local groups of other denominations have also held such meetings. One of these is Chapelwood Methodist Church in Houston, Texas, with the Rev. Grady Hardin as pastor at the time that the plan was instituted.

The practice of conducting retreats is more common among youth groups but is increasingly evident among young adults. Although such week-end meetings, usually held at some camp or assembly ground, often involve a great deal of recreation, the *koinonia* which emerges through worship, recreation, living together, and planning is often of a high order. Such retreats, especially among youth groups, usually consist of planning meetings, discussion groups, worship, and recreation. One mother reported that her teen-age daughter went to a retreat talking of the boys who were to be there but returned reporting on what the experience had meant to her religious life.

Another fairly common type of redemptive community in the United States is the youth work camp, at which a group of young people, usually college students, spend a summer or part of a summer carrying out a variety of activities in local churches or at other centers. Through their work and worship together, a level of *koinonia* not ordinarily experienced in the local church is often attained. It is conceivable that some modification of this plan might be feasible for adults.

On a larger scale the lay movement in Europe offers opportunities for deeper levels of fellowship, the best known of these centers being the Iona Community. Each summer on the tiny island where the ancient Iona Abbey was located, off the coast of Scotland, groups of ministers and laymen work and worship together. From their experiences here they return to their own parish churches to seek to deepen the spiritual life there.[23] Increasingly during recent years other centers have been established in Europe, including the Ecumenical Institute at Boissey, Switzerland, under the auspices of the World Council of Churches. Made possible by a gift from John D. Rockefeller, Jr., this center sponsors meetings for laymen to consider the Christian faith and its relation to their everyday life. They then return to their parishes to do much the same thing that members of the Iona Community do. The Evangelical Academies in Germany, the lay colleges in England, and many similar enterprises which are increasingly common in Europe, have been most adequately described in a pamphlet issued by the World Council of Churches called *Signs of Renewal: The Life of the Lay Institute in Europe*.[24]

In the United States centers similar to those in Europe have been established at Kirkridge, in Pennsylvania; at Brighton, Michigan (Parishfield); at Wallingsford, Pennsylvania (Pendle Hill); and in Richmond, Indiana (Quaker Hill).[25] The Christian Faith and Life Community in Austin, Texas, provides for students at The University of Texas living quarters, discussion groups, worship, and other activities aimed at awakening within the students deeper Christian understanding and commitment.[26]

Church Groups and Koinonia

These examples and types of groups which have been cited are only representative of what a local church, or the Church on a broader scope, can do in order to provide opportunities for the development of community among Christians. Both existing groups and newly formed groups ought to take seriously the help which comes to us from the fields of group work and group dynamics. Two warnings ought to be sounded, however: for one thing, as we have repeatedly said, Christian *koinonia* cannot be manufactured through the use of any or all techniques. It is the gift of God; yet man would be untrue to his destiny if he did not place himself in situations and utilize his understanding of how groups work in order to prepare the way for God's activity. His function is somewhat like that of John the Baptist: it is preparation, but it is he who cometh afterwards who speaks and acts the saving Word.

Second, we must beware lest the individual be lost even in our efforts to establish Christian community! There must always be freedom within fellowship.[27] The voice of the prophet must not be stilled. The will of the group is not necessarily the will of the Lord. The individual must at times stand against even the so-called Christian group.

Having heeded these warnings, however, the Christian is free to proceed on his work of preparation. It is especially important that the leader understand his role. The leader who dominates his group is, in a sense, himself playing god. He may easily stand between the persons for whom he has assumed responsibility and the God and Father of our Lord Jesus Christ. His role must be, to borrow a phrase, a *transparent* one.[28] As he seeks to work *with* persons rather than *for* them, as he seeks to share with them his own insights and knowledge rather than forcing these ideas upon them, he may become a human channel through whom the Spirit of God may work.

Jesus' promise in Matt. 18:20, "Where two or three are gathered in my name, there am I in the midst of them," is an open invitation for the Church and its leadership to encourage the togetherness of Christian men. True *koinonia*, let us say again, is the gift of God, but we can receive the gift only as we are prepared to do so. The small group in the Church is one of the ways in which this preparation can take place.

Thc Outreach of the Fellowship

A S WE HAVE ALREADY SEEN, A GROUP, BY ITS VERY NATURE, IS A collection of individuals which has developed a "we-feeling." Not until it has thus become *self*-conscious does it really become a group. Paul's description of the Church as the Body of Christ has sound sociological as well as theological foundations. Without pressing the analogy as far as some sociologists have done, it may be said that a group possesses many of the inner dynamics of the individual self, in that a kind of self-structure and unity must develop which sets it apart from, and often over against, other such groups. Just as individual selves, unless drawn together by such forces as fear or love, the need to belong or the need of self-fulfillment, may withdraw from each other, so groups, unless also propelled together by forces opposed to those which separate them, may pull apart. This is the familiar "in-group, out-group" phenomenon which has been described by sociologists.

Thus, while small groups seem necessary to provide a sense of belonging to individuals—indeed, for the development of the healthy self—they continually are tempted to exclusiveness. *My* group is set over against *your* group, *my* club against *yours*, *my* church against *yours*, *my* nation against *yours*. The divisiveness begins almost as soon as children develop group consciousness and continues throughout life. It is one of the most difficult phenomena to deal with whenever one is concerned with persons.

The Danger of Exclusiveness

Unfortunately, this human weakness manifests itself in the Church of Jesus Christ. True, wherever the Spirit of Christ is really at work, it is always effecting unity. But, as we have repeatedly said, the Church and its subgroups are both redeemed and being redeemed, and thus are subject to the same sins as non-Church groups.

In fact, it may well be that religious groups (both Christian and those belonging to other faiths) are subject to even greater dangers in this respect than nonreligious groups. This is due to the fact that the aims of religious groups are always given some ultimate reference, and thus to protect the interests of the group may become tantamount to defending the interests of what is considered ultimate in life. When a nation, such as Nazi Germany or Communist Russia, desires to insure final allegiance on the part of its citizenry, it often gives religious sanctions to its political aims. Indeed, it may be that "Americanism" has become for many people in the United States their real religion, whatever profession of allegiance they may give to Jesus Christ.

We are not surprised to find in the history of the Christian movement many examples of exclusiveness and self-centeredness. Whatever may have been its contributions throughout its history, the monastic movement, which provides the finest opportunity for close fellowship, has often been subject to pride and exclusiveness. As Richard Niebuhr has said, "Its intention was directed to the achievement of a Christian life, apart from civilization, in obedience to the laws of Christ, and in pursuit of a perfection wholly distinct from the aims that men seek in politics and economics, in sciences and arts." [1] Many of the orders performed acts of service in the larger society, but they were never really a part of that society, and some did not even do this.

The more exclusive Protestant sects, which also often maintain a high degree of inner fellowship and unity, likewise have been subject to pride and self-satisfaction. To quote Niebuhr again, "Hundreds of other groups, many of them evanescent, and thousands of individuals, have felt themselves compelled by loyalty to Christ to withdraw from culture and to give up all responsibility for the world." [2] To be sure, such groups are often strongly evangelistic but almost always in an individualistic manner.

Such an attitude toward life and culture has been characterized by Richard Niebuhr as the "Christ against culture" motif. This position may be briefly described as the attempt to reject all of life except that lived within the fellowship of one's particular group.[3] Perhaps John Bennett's term, "the strategy of withdrawal," [4] is even more descriptive. In any case the temptation is to turn in upon one's own group and to own no responsibility for anyone outside except as one feels a responsibility for bringing the favored few into the group. Such groups, either on a local or a more extensive level, tend to spend their energies working out their own salvation, unmindful or unconcerned about the teeming life about them.

It is not alone the sectarian group that faces this danger, however; the established denominations are also subject to it. Here it may take the form of pride in statistics, in denominational accomplishments, in invidious comparisons with other Christian groups not quite so prosperous. Whatever other barriers stand in the way of ecumenical unity, the psychosocial fact of in-group consciousness and pride in one's particular heritage is a formidable hindrance to Christian unity. Unfortunately, this denominational consciousness in some groups seems to be increasing, perhaps partly because of the threat which the ecumenical movement provides to such exclusiveness.

Further, this same sense of pride is a constant threat to the smaller groups and redemptive societies within the structure of the larger Church—local, denominational, or interdenominational. Pacifist groups, for example, have often been subject to this kind of self-righteousness, which is demonstrated by an attitude of disdain or mere tolerance for the nonpacifist. Some widely known prayer-group movements fall into the same trap, so that the nonmember may be considered as outside God's favor. Indeed, this danger must be kept in mind by any concerned group.

The Group Turned Outward

What has been said is not to argue against the concerned group, for whenever the Spirit of Christ has really entered into the life of such a group, it will inevitably be turned outward, as, indeed, monasticism at its best has been. "He who finds his life will lose it, and he who loses his life for my sake will find it" (Matt. 10:39) is the word of Scripture to both individual and group. It is the very essence of the Christian gospel that the follower of Christ must turn his face outward. God has brought health and salvation to him; now he must be an instrument through which the Good News may be broadcast to others. (See, for example, Rom. 10:8-14; II Cor. 5:17-20.) The person who has responded to the love of God in Christ has no alternative except to seize every means available to reach his hand out to his brother.

This means that on a practical level the purpose of Christian *koinonia* is twofold: to encourage spiritual maturity on the part of those within the fellowship, and to serve as a leaven for the entire lump, or all of society. Whatever may have been in the past, or may be in the future, the values of the various motifs by which the Christian meets the world (such motifs being partially conditioned by the nature of the culture in which he lives), it would appear that the only adequate expression of the relationship of Church and world in *our* culture is that contained in Richard Niebuhr's phrase, "Christ the transformer of culture." [5] In other words, the individual Christian and the Christian group must turn outward to the life about them and be concerned with its every aspect.

We have already implied—but it must be stated and explicated— that the reverse of this proposition is also significant: namely, the Christian's outreach, be it through evangelism, missions, social service, or Christian action, must come out of his central commitment and not be conceived in legalistic-humanitarian terms, as the so-called "social gospel" of the early twentieth century tended to be. The Christian's concern is not *primarily* humanitarian, though he is the most humanitarian of persons. His impetus comes not from a "feeling" of kindness toward all mankind; his is a more fundamental motive, his response to almighty God. He does not promote works of welfare and social improvement because he thinks human beings are *worthy* of such works; rather, his knowledge of *his own* unworthiness of God's love plus his assurance that God loves all men regardless of how *unworthy* they may be, leads him to do so. In other words, he acts because of who he is.

There is a profound insight contained in the parable of the Prodigal Son which we usually miss. Most of us, whether we recognize it or not, identify with the elder brother, because from all *human* perspectives he was right! He might have tolerated (and so might we) the reception of the prodigal son had the father executed judgment by making him one of the hired servants. The elder brother was not callous, as we sometimes make him, nor are most of us. But he could not understand why the father provided a party for the son who had thrown away his money and the best years of his life. Neither can we, for this is the bestowing of favor where favor is not due. Thus it is easy for our "charity," since it so often involves persons who are not worthy of favor because they have little "dignity" left, to grow cold. It is no wonder that social workers whose only motivation is humanitarian sometimes become hard and calloused. So will our "outreach" become conventional, imperialistic, or condescending if our recognition of *our* unworthiness, of *our* need of forgiveness, of *our* reception of God's grace freely given, is not continually renewed.

Thus, we must return for the moment to the concept discussed in Chap. V. The vocation (call) of the individual—and consequently of the group—is to serve God. We serve God through worship but also through acts of love and concern for our fellow men. God calls us through his redeeming love; love of life and love of fellow men are possible because I am loved of God.[6] "Not that I have already obtained this or am already perfect," writes Paul, "but I press on to make it my own, *because Christ Jesus has made me his own.*" (Phil. 3:12, italics mine.)

This is the heart of the Christian gospel. It is also the theme of perhaps the most important document of the Christian heritage, Paul's letter to the Romans. It was partly the elaborate sacrificial and ceremonial practices of Judaism and other religions against which Paul was writing, but his word is relevant to us for other reasons. Men had come to think that they could win the favor of God by engaging in these elaborate ceremonies and in the keeping of the Law. (See especially Rom. 2:12–4:25.) Today, church people are just as prone to believe that *they* can win God's favor, except they have substituted moral acts and good works for the ceremonial practices of older religions. If we only tithe, we will receive God's favor. If we are "good," we will earn our way to heaven. If we will only do good to others, our salvation is assured. If we will only work a little harder, we may even be able to contribute to the building of God's Kingdom.

This is a far cry from the word of Scripture on the basis of salvation, and it is quite different from the Christian motivation for the outreach of the Church with which we are concerned in this chapter. The Christian loves because God first loved him; he acts because God has acted in Christ; he forgives because he knows God has first forgiven him. God has already taken the initiative: man only responds. The Christian does not reach out to others *in order to win God's favor* but because *God has already shown this favor* in Christ. This means that nothing that is said in the following pages concerning *means* of outreach should be interpreted as a set of legalistic instructions for the Christian to follow in order to be a Christian. Rather, they must be seen in relation to all that has previously been said. Such acts *grow out of* the Christian's response to God.

Just as we have said that the motivation for outreach and service is the Christian's response to God, we have also said that this response inevitably means outreach and service. Let us look at some of the means by which this can be done in our modern world.

Service Within the Fellowship

Let us begin with that which is common and obvious: namely, *the service done by members within their own fellowship.* A perennial problem of Protestant churches, for example, is securing workers in the church school. Having taken seriously the concept of the lay ministry, we are confronted with the difficulty of finding leaders who are committed Christians, aware of the meanings of the Christian faith, able to communicate by relationship, word, and deed, the meaning of the gospel, willing to work at being adequate for their task.

Take as a single example the desperate need for adequate adult leaders of young people. In many churches the youth program is either ineffective or almost nonexistent. It is not easy to work with teen-agers, especially in the early years of that period. There are many competing interests for young people today. Perhaps no one has a solution to the youth problem either in the Church or the larger society. There are enough instances of effective youth programs, however, to assure us that it is not really a *youth* problem, but actually an *adult* problem. Wherever there is effective, committed adult leadership, willing to work with young people in creative and dynamic relationships, something is happening.

As an approach to this problem, one church set up a special class for potential youth teachers to run for fifteen weeks. The approach was not the traditional one, "We will offer you some techniques, some 'methods of working with young people,' which will make you a successful youth worker." Rather the first five weeks were spent in exploring the modern approach to the Bible and its central themes. The second period was occupied with major Christian beliefs. Only in the last five weeks was there any direct reference to teaching as such, and here the emphasis was on so understanding young people as to make the gospel relevant to their lives. It is this approach which is most likely to develop genuine concern for working with youth, not reluctant assent in doing a job.

Besides the more commonly thought-of areas of work (such as administration, teaching, serving as officers of various groups, and the like), there are new frontiers of parish activity. Included in these would be service to older adults, both those confined to their homes and those able to participate in limited parish activities; the organization and oversight of community groups where the boundaries of the parish are extensive; the extension of the services of the Church to parents; the leading of small study and prayer groups such as were described in the previous chapter; the pioneering in other ways so as to deepen the spiritual life of the congregation. Both the routine work of the congregation and the more exciting pioneering are necessary parts of the ongoing life of a local fellowship. Here are opportunities for a wide range of interests and abilities to be expressed by the committed Christian.

Evangelism

It is not alone the interior life of the congregation which calls for individual and group participation, however; the congregation must continually be reaching out beyond its geographical center in a church building by many ways, including *evangelism*. The Christian church is by its very nature evangelistic; the smaller group within the larger fellowship must also be concerned with others. Having been grasped by the message of the gospel, the Christian's first impulse should be to seek ways of sharing the Good News with his brothers.

Unfortunately much evangelistic effort of recent years has been too much centered in "getting new members." Statistics have received far too much emphasis, and the growth of membership has sometimes been substituted for the winning of persons to Christ and the upbuilding of his Body. Laymen must understand more fully the nature of the evangelistic task. When they do, some who are now active in "fishermen's clubs" and similar organizations will drop by the wayside, but others will no doubt respond with greater zeal. Further, a reconstitution of the evangelistic program will take cognizance of the fact that evangelism is much more than calling on prospective members, that it is fundamentally the witnessing of Christians in their daily lives to the power of the gospel.

Paul Tillich has put the evangelistic motive in profound perspective in his sermon, "The New Being." After pointing out the danger that church members will glory in church organization, religious structures, and membership statistics (which he identifies with what Paul means when he speaks of "circumcision," or an outward sign or form, in Gal. 6:15), he goes on to say that the heart of the gospel is that God through Christ will renew our old being into something new when we respond to his love and forgiveness. Then he asks the question, "How shall Christianity face the secular movements, other religions, and the

129

various faiths which confront it in the modern world?" In other words, what shall be its evangelistic motive?

Shall Christianity tell them: Come to us, we are a better religion, our kind of circumcision or uncircumcision is higher than yours? Shall we praise Christianity, our way of life, the religious as well as the secular? Shall we make of the Christian message a success story, and tell them, like advertisers: try it with us, and you will see how important Christianity is for everybody?[7]

This, he feels, is the approach of some ministers, missionaries, and laymen, but it ought not to be. Rather we ought to say to these people:

Don't compare your religion and our religion, your rites and our rites, your prophets and our prophets, your priests and our priests, the pious amongst you, and the pious amongst us. . . . Don't think we want to convert you to English or American Christianity, to the religion of the Western World. We do not want to convert you to us, not even to the best of us. . . . We want only to show you something we have seen and to tell you something we have heard: That in the midst of the old creation there is a New Creation, and that this New Creation is manifest in Jesus who is called the Christ.[8]

Not only in motive but also in method does change need to take place in our evangelism. There is undoubtedly a place for religious surveys and organized "campaigns" of mass and visitation evangelism. Further, there is real hope in what has been called "fellowship evangelism," which consists of bringing unchurched folk into the fellowship of a Church group (such as a Sunday-school class) in an effort to win them to discipleship through the love and concern manifest in the fellowship.[9] But these are not enough. The new emphasis on the witness of the Christian in his total life, especially in daily work, is an area which is receiving new attention.

Reference has already been made to the current insights available in this relation.[10] At the 1954 meeting of the Assembly of the World Council of Churches, one entire study group was devoted to evangelism. The concluding statement of the document prepared for this group lifts up this new emphasis:

Evengelism is the participation of the total Christian community in Christ's mission in the world;

Every single aspect of the Church's life and activities is of evangelistic significance;

In proclamation, fellowship and service, the Church must demonstrate the Gospel in the actual life context of men;

Laymen are on the frontline, served by the ministry whose function is to equip the people of God for its mission.

Laity and ministry together strive to be of the mind of Him who "emptied Himself" in service to the world.[11]

Of equal importance at this same meeting is the fact that another study, "The Laity—the Christian in His Vocation," also made much of the evangelistic mission of the laity in their daily life. In a statement previously quoted occur these words: "It is in the life and work of the lay membership that the Church must manifest in the world its regenerative and redemptive power. One of the greatest tasks of the Church today is to grasp clearly the significance of the lay ministry *in* the world." [12] This statement was made with the recognition that there are millions of persons in the so-called Christian West who have no contact with the organized Church and are not likely to come under its influence unless Christian laymen who work alongside them in factory, office, and market place witness to them. Such witnessing must be done according to strategies which we are only beginning to develop.

What is called for here is the approach previously described in relation to the group which developed in a British church. Here, it will be remembered, a small group formed themselves together as a result of an evangelistic mission in which they had engaged. Their first concern was to understand more fully the meaning of their own discipleship. When this need was partially met and they began to see more clearly the nature of their responsibility, they were ready to reach out to others. Out of a deepened concern came a more profound conception of what an evangelist is and does.[13]

Service and Action

A *third* means of outreach into the community is that of *service and action*. Here too new modes of expression are needed. Often the "social service" of the Church is restricted to collecting baskets of food at Thanksgiving and Christmas and to dealing with various emergencies. Quite often such service is rendered in a condescending manner. However helpful such acts may be in alleviating temporary

131

need, they are inadequate. Even the support of such causes as homes for children, for unmarried mothers, and for the aged; provision of relief through such organizations as CARE, CROP, and church relief agencies; and the giving to many worthy causes, while all worth while, should not be considered as complete expressions of the *agape* which permeates the Christian fellowship. In other words, ways must be found of expressing on a more profound level the love of neighbor commanded by Jesus, without neglecting such expressions as are listed above.

Too often, in fact, our modern social service is carried on without personal involvement of the giver. "We've given to the orphans' home; we've given to the Community Chest; we even support missions— that ought to be enough." "The gift without the giver is bare" is as true as it was when James Russell Lowell wrote the lines. The giving of one's self in service is the Christian measure of the depth of the act.

As one of the means by which this may be accomplished, the work camp may be mentioned. Although it is usually carried out by young people, there is no reason why it could not be adopted for adult use. As a matter of fact, the old practice of the neighbors' helping out in an emergency (such as the illness of the breadwinner) was a fore-runner of the modern work camp. A local church might spend a Saturday working on a community project, even though it was something as "secular" as building a baseball diamond. As a single example, several church-school classes of young couples in one church became interested in the possibilities which existed in a mission church in a poor section of the city. It did not seem sufficient simply to give money to the church. Therefore, on several occasions class members spent Saturday afternoon working on the physical properties of the mission. Others have helped on various occasions in the leadership of activities at the project. One individual, skilled as a mechanic, provided a castoff automobile and his own skill in assisting boys of the community to learn the work of a mechanic.

On a large scale such experiments as the East Harlem Protestant Parish in New York City and the West Side Mission in Chicago point in the direction of a more complete witness to the untouched community in both faith and action. In New York City a group of concerned ministers and theological students have been carrying on since 1948 a project which, though centered in the Church, seeks to reach out into the total community and touch the lives of people at points

132

where they are concerned existentially. Matters of rent, tenement improvement, general community uplift, and similar concerns are taken as seriously as the building of a church membership.[14] More recently such a project has also been started in Chicago.[15] Both of these projects are located in areas of extreme poverty, a fact which conditions greatly the type of ministry they carry on. The basic principle on which they operate seems sound, however: the responsibility of the local church to minister to its total community. The more normal pattern in Protestantism, however, has been for the local congregation to ignore the immediate community when it begins to deteriorate and to continue to serve members from "better" areas of the city, or to move out.

Not only should the "service areas" of the Church include the immediate community in which it is located; it ought to extend to the total areas of social, economic, and political life. Wherever such a statement is made, the cry of "meddling" is usually raised. Yet if one takes seriously the mission of Christ to all of life he can hardly ignore all social problems. The Church, to use a familiar figure, must not only be at the foot of the cliff with an ambulance ready to pick up those who fall off; it must also help build a fence at the top of the cliff to prevent persons from falling off.

A problem of concern for the present is the efforts made to integrate the Negro into full participation in the life of the nation. Legislation can create the conditions under which integration can come to pass, but the process of integration is one which involves education and the dealing with points of tension. The establishment of law is only a step, and the work of the Church must continue after this condition has come about.[16] Such work is fraught with difficulties, disappointments, and criticism, and Christians will obviously not agree as to the solution to particular problems. Not to show concern over such matters and not to work toward the solution of these problems is to risk making the Church of Jesus Christ an *exclusive* rather than an *inclusive* society, however.

The need for careful and prayerful dealing with social issues is illustrated in the following approach:[17]

1. The first step is *to secure and make known the facts involved in the situation.* For example, in one urban community where organized opposition to the United Nations was increasing a few years ago, an interested group dedicated themselves to the securing and disseminating of facts about the United Nations and its affiliate organizations.

A speakers' bureau was organized and information about available speakers was sent to community and church organizations. Numerous speeches were made, and newspaper articles informed the larger public. The co-operation of many agencies, including churches, helped to turn the tide from opposition to reasonably informed acceptance.

In the matter of integration, knowledge of how it has worked,[18] information about the Negro group, and statements from persons and groups favoring integration may help in the process. In some community it may take long and patient effort before this can be brought about.

2. Along with the positive matter of the dissemination of information, one must also *be able to answer the questions of the opposition.* In the case of the United Nations group, a serious effort was made in dealing with questions raised by groups to which speakers went concerning the alleged disloyalty of UN employees, the "godlessness" of UNESCO, and the threat to the sovereignty of the United States. Usually such answers will not silence the vocal opposition, but they may satisfy many who are neither for nor against, but are wavering in their attitude.

One such question that must be dealt with in the matter of integration concerns intermarriage. It is important to have information concerning the low incidence of interracial marriages in communities where integration has existed for many years.

3. *Action should be attempted in areas where reasonable success can be expected.* The UN group, for example, brought Henry Cabot Lodge to the city for a public address. Since there was no basis on which even the reactionary group could question the loyalty of Ambassador Lodge, such a meeting could be expected to receive public acceptance and good press coverage.

In the case of integration, those dealing with a particular community must know at what points that community is ready to accept change. To hurry the matter may be to risk the gains of the past. There comes a time when, in any campaign, the results of the past must be consolidated. A method of "cautious advance," which involves both *caution* and *advance* has been advocated as the approach especially appropriate to the Southern community.[19]

4. *The Church can co-operate with other agencies unless the motives of these agencies are wrong.* The qualifying phrase seems necessary, since one of the mistakes made by those interested in social action

between the two World Wars was that they co-operated with Communist front organizations even when their basic motives were in disagreement. Motives and basic orientations must always be examined by Christians. In the case of the UN group (referred to above), Unitarians, Protestants, Roman Catholics, and Jews, along with those not concerned with any religious motivation, were able to work together since their motives were not basically out of harmony with one another. In the case of race relations, the Church often finds nonchurch agencies doing more than it is. The least it can do is to work alongside those agencies whose basic orientation is not opposed to its own, and to co-operate where this seems advisable.

5. *The Christian must continue to be sensitive to the implications of his faith in all areas of social and economic life and to fulfill his responsibility as an individual Christian and as a member of the Christian community in every way possible.* This means continued study of social and political matters. It means prophetic preaching. It necessitates small study groups considering the meaning of the gospel in both general and specific areas of society. Christians will not agree on these questions, though they must learn to disagree in love. The minister in Protestantism cannot dictate to the conscience of the laity, though he ought to witness concerning his convictions. He is not a specialist in economics or politics, but he does need to have enough basic information about these and other areas that he can seek to relate the Christian faith to these issues. But it is really up to the laity, as we have already seen, to be a constructive force in these areas. It is usually he who must hold office, who must make decisions in business, who must witness to his faith in his daily work. Thus, the leadership of the Church must provide the kind of help which will make it possible for laymen to understand the implications of their faith for daily living and must give them the kind of reinforcement for living courageously that encourages action in society.

"Missions"

Let us move now to a fourth area of outreach, namely that which is usually called *"missions."* It would be well if this term could be dropped altogether, since it tends to differentiate between the task of the Church in the so-called "Christian lands" and in the non-Christian, or between that which it does in the "normal" parish and that which it does in special situations, such as in the slums or with the Indian

Americans. Likewise it still has the connotation of condescension to many. Actually the so-called program of "missions" of the Christian Church is nothing more nor less than the program for implementing the world-wide *mission* of the Church. "Go therefore and make disciples of all nations." Matt. 28:19*a* is the Christian imperative.

Much rethinking of how this mission should be expressed in our day has occurred during recent years, but the essential imperative remains clear.[20] The modern mission of the Church is to the family next door, and to the family across the ocean; to organized labor, and to capital; to the underprivileged of our own city and to the overprivileged; to the illiterate and to the highly educated; to the rural areas of America and to the villages of India; to the exploited in Latin America and to the rulers of Soviet Russia—indeed to all men everywhere who have not heard, or having heard have not responded to, the gospel of Christ. The means of this mission will vary, but they will include all desirable media: means of combating illiteracy, ways of improving agricultural production, the healing of disease, the teaching of the superior as well as the inferior, the proclamation of the gospel, and the building up of the Fellowship—but it will not forget its unique contribution, which is the communication of a person, God as revealed in Jesus Christ. This is the real mission of the Church, at home and abroad.

How can the local congregation participate? We have already considered ways by which it can minister to its own community and to the larger society of which it is a part. With respect to those separated geographically, the contribution of financial means for making the communication possible is central. It can also contribute through the giving of its young people to the enterprise. Above all, the local congregation must keep alive to the breadth of the task which is ours and be aware of its responsibility unto the least and the last of these our brethren.

The Ecumenical Movement

One further type of outreach may be mentioned briefly, the Ecumenical Movement and its various organizations on local, national, and world levels. Many Christians believe that the ecumenical movement (that is, the spirit drawing Christians of various persuasions into co-operative discussion and action) is nothing less than the work of the Holy Spirit in the Church today. The various organizations, such as local and state councils of churches, the National Council of Churches, and the World Council of Churches, are important, but it is the movement itself which is the most noteworthy. At times such organizations may actually stand in the way of the movement, though they are necessary expressions of it.

So significant is this movement that it is quite probable that the Christian who supports it by word and deed is participating in a reformation of the Church as far-reaching as the Protestant Reformation of the fifteenth and sixteenth centuries. A host of questions concerning interchurch unity are yet to be answered, but the spirit of unity does exist. Through participation in an organization which seeks to implement this spirit on any level, the layman or minister may have a share in effecting larger areas of real co-operation and union.

The Church's Mission

In a sense all that has been written in this chapter is superfluous, provided the earlier chapters are taken seriously. If the Church is true to its divine mission and if individual Christians seek to implement that mission, the Church will be a fellowship that reaches out beyond its own confines and expresses this mission. Yet because of the danger that we shall become so concerned with working out our own salvation that we forget those beyond our fellowship, we must be continually reminded of this larger responsibility. The local congregation or denomination which fails to keep the larger concern before itself is in danger of the sin of exclusiveness. For the sake of its own health, as well as for the sake of others, and pre-eminently because its Lord demands it, the congregation or the smaller group within the congregation must turn its thinking outward to the great world beyond, to the multitudes for whom Christ died and whom he seeks to win today.

X

Providing Leadership for the Fellowship

O NE OF THE CRUCIAL PROBLEMS THAT ARISES WHEN THE CHURCH is taken seriously as the People of God is that of providing adequate lay leadership. If we understand the Church in terms of universal priesthood and *koinonia*, then we cannot be satisfied with clerical and professional leadership alone. In a real sense each participating member of the community is a potential leader. Yet in our complex culture, the demands made upon leadership are such that a high degree of understanding of both the nature and mission of the Church, along with skill in performing a particular job, is necessary for satisfactory leadership. The matter to which we now turn our attention is thus of both unusual significance and challenge.

The Danger of "Professionalism"

There seems to be no great danger that American Protestantism will fall victim of the kind of *clericalism* which has already been noted as being characteristic of both Roman Catholicism and Protestantism in Europe. There is a tendency, however, when the church is thought of primarily as *organization* or *institution,* for *professionalism* to develop. With the tremendous increase of the number of members of national board staffs, and with the growth of the multiple ministry in the local church, there is the perennial temptation for the American Church to rely more and more on these professional (paid) workers. On the national scale, the board executives—the civil service corps of the church as they have been called—have become increasingly powerful in the formulation of program and policy for major denominations. In local churches, particularly when one or more additional workers are employed besides the principal pastor, laymen are often tempted to allow the paid staff to "run the church."

Indeed, in a few local churches this trend has gone so far that most, or even all, of the educational leadership is paid. Some religious educators a few years back openly advocated the employment of such leadership where possible. With the conception of the church which

138

has been presented in previous pages, however, this move must be called into question.

That there are many problems involved in lay leadership for the Church is freely admitted. No doubt churches that have paid teachers, or even paid supervisors and leading teachers, have educational programs that are more efficiently administered and teaching that is more educationally sound. Yet, if the point of view expressed in the opening chapters of this book is valid, the additional efficiency and competence are not sufficient to make up for what is lost. When the Church is thought of fundamentally as a Fellowship of Faith, it is doubtful if paid leadership on such an extensive scale can be justified.

Indeed, if the principle of the priesthood of believers is taken in utter seriousness, the teaching function of the Church cannot even be relegated to those especially chosen for specific teaching tasks. Rather, "Responsibility for teaching rests upon the whole church even though only certain members undertake specific teaching assignments." [1] Then the function of paid workers, be they ordained clergymen or trained professional Christian educators, is to be assistants to the voluntary leadership of the Church. This point of view was expressed more than a quarter of a century ago by one of the pioneers in modern religious education when he insisted that the professional worker ought to be employed to "inspire and train" lay workers for the fellowship of teaching, "to discover, organize and use their talents and abilities; to set them an example of how their special parts in the total program may be carried on—in a word, to multiply rather than to subtract from lay leadership possibilities." [2]

The Protestant movement in twentieth-century America needs to examine itself carefully with respect to the danger of professionalism.

The Nature of Leadership

A further factor bearing on leadership has to do with one's conception of the role of the leader, be he ordained or lay. This was discussed in a previous chapter[3] and it was insisted that the role of the leader is not to dominate or dictate but rather to guide, encourage, suggest, and give counsel. Specifically the role of the *teacher* is to witness to his own faith, transmitting the heritage which is his to share and seeking to evoke from others a personal response to the God who is revealed through that heritage.

What we have been saying is that one's conception of his leadership role ought to be consistent with his belief about the Church, its ministry, and its offices. *Leadership should grow out of faith.* This has something to say about the *motives of leadership.* Too much of the leadership of local parishes is carried on because of a sense of duty, a desire for recognition, the satisfaction of ego needs, or some other unworthy or inadequate motive. Actually leadership ought to emerge out of the fellowship, to arise as a natural expression of faith. When it does so, then it may be thought of as "natural" rather than "forced." Leadership for the Fellowship must always come out of commitment if it is to be Christian in quality.

In other words the committed Christian will be on the lookout for opportunities suited to his abilities through which he may express his concern and carry out his vocation (call) as a Christian. This will include not only leadership within the Fellowship but also, as was pointed out in the preceding chapter, in the larger community. The principle involved in lay teaching, as well as in the filling of administrative posts and other assignments, is the Protestant principle of a universal and mutual priesthood.

Enlisting Lay Leadership

Ideally, then, any emphasis on recruiting leadership ought to be secondary to a call to commitment. Under such conditions a *program of enlistment* of lay leadership would hardly be necessary, with a presentation of opportunities for service being sufficient. Actually, however, the call to Christian commitment has too often been presented without reference to the responsibilities attendant to the acceptance of God's love and forgiveness. Further, even when the two are related, some additional incentive is probably needed to secure a particular person for a particular position. Hence some kind of enlistment program is required.

Such a program will consist of the usual means: personal calls on new members asking them to indicate areas where they would like to serve; the presentation of leadership needs to adult groups in the church, such as adult church-school classes, the women's group, the men's club, and the like; personal contacts with persons who appear to have special contributions to make to the life of the church; and a continuous emphasis on the place of service in Christian commitment. A special committee, or an individual in smaller churches, is often appointed to carry through this program.

Occasionally churches will do well to carry out a special program of enlistment. One church organized such a campaign as carefully as it organizes its financial drive. Teams were appointed to call in homes, with the captains of teams responsible to group captains, who in turn were responsible to the campaign leader. It was determined that the appeal would be made to parents of children in the church school, and the slogan selected was, "Take your turn." A simple card was provided on which the interests of each person could be listed. These cards were entered in a permanent file when interest was shown, so that follow-up at a later time might actually result in enlisting the worker. A year later the campaign was repeated, with another set of prospects used.

Perhaps the most important practical word to be said is that an emphasis on enlistment must be continuous, not sporadic, even if special campaigns are occasionally carried out. A further word of warning must be issued: namely, in any emphasis on enlistment, the motivation which has already been described must be kept central. Just as effective leadership comes out of commitment, so a call to service is also a call to deepened commitment.

The Necessity for an Educated Leadership

Not only is there a need for a continuous emphasis on enlistment; there is also a need for a continuous program of leadership education. This is necessary, practically, because the church is inevitably compared with other community institutions. As the quality of teaching in public schools has improved, for example, it has become more urgent that teaching in the church improve. As community agencies acquire new understandings of the functioning of groups, it becomes necessary for the church to utilize this new knowledge in its own interior life.

There is a second, and more profound, reason for this, however—namely, leadership must come out of an *informed* commitment. Lay leadership which is uninformed simply perpetuates the mistaken notions of the past. The intellectual illumination of the meaning of faith in a world where competing ideologies are attractively and alluringly present is no longer an option, to be given primarily to students in theological seminaries. It is important that the "average" layman have some intelligent comprehension of what it means to live as a Christian in the twentieth century; it is an absolute requirement that the layman who works with children, youth, and adults in a leadership role have this prerequisite.

Indeed, if the Church is to be a real fellowship, if it is to manifest the priesthood of the laity, commitment in terms of a nineteenth-century understanding of the Christian faith will never do. We must take seriously the matter of calling not only for committed leadership but also for informed leadership. The implementation of all which has been written in these pages is dependent upon this central fact.

Yet it can be safely said that Protestantism has not adopted a total strategy for the education of lay leadership. When it does so, it will work toward a strategy which includes a total adult-education program with special consideration to the needs of parents, teachers and other church-school leaders, administrative officials, officers of the various organizations, ushers, members of the choir, lay speakers, church visitors, lay evangelists, lay counselors, leaders of worship, those concerned with witnessing in their daily work, those interested in community service and action—the entire range of workers both within the Fellowship and within the larger community of which the Church is a part.

Education in the Christian Heritage

With what has been said about the importance of leadership education in mind, let us turn to a consideration of the types of education which such leaders ought to have. The *first* of these is that which has already been mentioned, namely, a serious consideration of *the meaning of the Christian faith* as it is related to life in the twentieth century.

Nothing that was said in the chapter on nurture was intended to minimize the importance of the ideas which belong to the Christian heritage. Christian nurture, to be sure, is much broader than the passing on of facts, ideas, and materials. Yet the Christian faith does have a subject matter which can be fairly clearly delineated, and the failure to understand this heritage means that Elton Trueblood's characterization of lay preaching as often consisting of "no more than a string of sloppily quoted Biblical phrases, linked together by commonplace ideas" [4] is equally true of much lay teaching.

What, then, are the major areas of the subject matter of the Christian faith? The *Bible* will naturally be the basis for a study of the Christian heritage. It does not seem possible to take the Bible seriously in the twentieth century without taking into account the approach to it which has been wrought out by scholars during the last century. Yet this knowledge has scarcely begun to be made known to laymen.

142

Since many ministers still fear the results of a frank consideration with laymen of the results of this painstaking study of the Bible, they often neglect the Bible in both preaching and teaching, being willing neither to propound the older literalistic view nor to venture forth with the new. It is probably not too strong a statement to say that the far too common attitude of laymen toward the Bible is that it is an ancient book which has *some* reference to the Christian faith but which is not to be taken really seriously. Only as the Bible is studied and taught from the modern point of view is it likely to become a living book to modern man (and thus a medium of God's revelation to him).

This is not to suggest an immediate shattering of the bibliolatry of those churchmen who do, to some extent, take the Bible seriously. Nor is it meant to advocate the presentation to laymen of the details of textual, historical, and form criticism. Such an approach as is found in Floyd V. Filson's *Opening the New Testament* [5] or in *The Interpreter's Bible* [6] is intended. A serious consideration of such works ought to increase the faith of laymen rather than to shatter it, since we have entered a day when biblical criticism is seen as a tool, not an end in itself.

Both of these resources—Filson's brief book and the comprehensive *Interpreter's Bible*—point to the reading and study of the Bible itself. We shall continue to need teaching *about* the Bible which presents background, problems of date and authorship, answers to problems involving sources, style, and language, and the like, but all of this must be pointed in one direction: that the biblical message itself may be understood.

Further, the biblical message must be presented so that it becomes relevant to human existence today. This is not to imply that there are simple answers to present-day problems. Many modern situations were unknown in biblical times, and there is always the danger that we will seek a "proof text" in answer to problems with which the Bible does not even deal. Further, our questions are not always proper ones, and often it is the Bible which suggests the question we ought to ask as well as the "answer." Yet this "method of correlation," to use Tillich's phrase,[7] is essential to an understanding of the Bible if it is to become God's living word to us today.[8] The teacher must be helped, therefore, not only to understand the background and content of the Bible but also to see the relation of the biblical message for today. This is a tremendous undertaking, but nothing less than this is sufficient for adequately prepared leaders in the Church.

Another area of the Christian heritage which must be included in our training for lay leaders is *the nature and history of the Church*, including one's own denomination. This cannot be disassociated from theology, nor can it be separated from a study of the Bible. The history of the Christian community is a continuation of the history of God's dealing with Israel, as recorded in the Old Testament. The Church, whose history begins in the New Testament, continues to the present day, and God's revelation of himself does not stop with the end of the Bible. Thus the history of the Church since biblical times must be viewed as the continuing activity of God through the Holy Spirit. In presenting this panorama of the Church, an elementary book like Roland H. Bainton's *The Church of Our Fathers* [9] is a good place to begin. On a somewhat more advanced level is Dillenberger and Welch's consideration of Protestantism, *Protestant Christianity*.[10] Through these and more advanced works the church leader may be made aware of the continuing heritage which is his.

A third area of the content of the Christian faith consists of *theology*, or Christian beliefs. In this realm also far-reaching changes have been taking place during recent decades, these changes having scarcely gone beyond the theological seminary. For fifty years prior to about 1930 a type of theology which de-emphasized the sovereignty of God and underemphasized the sinfulness of man prevailed in the "liberal" churches. Partly as a reaction to this thinking, fundamentalism, which is literalistic in its approach to the Bible and bases its theological thinking on a pre-twentieth-century scientific framework, arose. Many modern churchmen find it impossible to assume either of these positions, and a third type of thinking has arisen for which there is no adequate title, though it is often known as "neo-orthodoxy." Many who have been affected by Barth, Brunner, and Reinhold Niebuhr, the pioneers of the "new theology," would prefer to be called "neo-liberal," and others prefer to have no label at all. In spite of many disagreements, there is common ground in this theological approach.

Taking into full account both the findings of modern biblical study and the fact that our science and psychology are quite different from those in which the biblical revelation occurred, these theologians have reasserted the major doctrine of Christian theology, often reinterpreting them and restating them in modern terminology but reaffirming the normative nature of the biblical revelation, especially as found in Jesus Christ. "Modern orthodoxy," to quote Hordern, "believes that in the orthodox tradition we have a previous heritage of truth which must not be thrown overboard just because someone has split the atom and someone else has looked farther through a telescope." [11] It is this type of theology which Elton Trueblood has designated one of the "signs of hope" [12] in the modern Church. In this period of theological revival, it is of utmost importance that those in positions of lay leadership be provided with a deeper understanding of the faith of the Christian community.

One of the dangers which some observers fear in the new theology is the possibility that too little emphasis will be placed on the nature of the Christian life, or ethics. Opposed as it is to the moralism and "do-goodism" of liberalism, the newer theological thinking does seem at times to place too little emphasis on personal and social ethics. This fear is not justified, however, when the relationship between faith and ethics is understood. Faith is prior to action; theology stands behind Christian living, as we have repeatedly said. God's action precedes man's response. As Hordern has put it, "The living of Christianity is primary. Before thought there comes the experience of being a Christian. . . . Theology becomes thinking about life and its problems in the light of the fact that one is a Christian." [13] Life precedes theology, and theology must always be related to the problems of existence, which are ethical as well as theological. In every situation, one must ask, "What is my response to God here and now?"

Therefore a fourth emphasis is our course of study for laymen is the nature of the Christian life, or Christian ethics, personal and social. It is obviously easier in this regard to teach a set of moral principles, or laws, than it is to discuss the ethical implications of the Christian faith in concrete situations. When the ethical task is conceived as that of providing a set of principles, however, it leads to some new legalism. Hence, the ethical task of our generation is not an easy one; yet education for laymen, as we have repeatedly said in previous chapters, must include this matter of seeing the meaning of the Christian faith in all of life's relationships.

A fifth emphasis which ought to be made is the meaning and purpose of Christian worship. Since this has been considered in a complete chapter,[14] it will not be pursued further here.

Toward Understanding the Human Self

As the first area of study for laymen consists of the nature of the Christian faith, so the *second* concerns *the human self*, both as subject and object: that is, an understanding of one's self and of others. This is obviously too vast an area to discuss here. Some general principles relative to self-understanding and understanding those with whom one works have been suggested in preceding chapters, especially with respect to the social nature of the self, the way in which learning takes place, and the nature of group life. All leaders in the Church who work with other people—and this includes almost everyone—need as much of this understanding as possible. It is not alone an understanding *in general* but also an appreciation of the *specific* characteristics of an age group and the particular qualities of the group with which one is working. Teaching must continually move back and forth between the Christian faith itself and the persons involved if it is to be effective.

Further, the worker in the Church needs to understand the human person as he is viewed theologically, as well as psychologically. To recognize the simple facts of human nature, with its tendency toward self-assertion and its insecurity in the face of frustration, is to take a step toward understanding one's self and others. To remember that human behavior may be partially understood in terms of its immediate and deeper causes is to make progress in learning to work with others. But the Christian must go a step further and see both himself and his neighbor as sinner. To know one's self as a *forgiven sinner* is even more important. Indeed, this may be the beginning of fellowship. To be humble in one's estimate of himself and to be charitable in one's appraisals of others is to begin to know the nature of the Christian faith. All of this must be part of the understanding of the persons who seek to work with others in the Christian fellowship.

Understanding the Nature of Leadership

A *third* major area of concern in our program of leadership education is *the nature of leadership*. Since this has been considered in other places, it needs only an additional word here. The experience of democratic participation is necessary in the developing of democratic leadership. It is the responsibility of ministers, directors of religious education, and other professional leaders to provide such experience in their leadership of groups. The experience of being a part of a loving, accepting group is the basis for being a loving, accepting leader.

Education in Methodology

(4) A *fourth* emphasis should be on *methodology,* or the means of performing a particular task. Such methodology must always be seen in the perspective of the meaning of the Christian faith and the nature of the Church. Too often method has been divorced from content. Yet the purpose of method is simply to bridge the gap between theory and practice, between faith and action. For example, a church usher must have some understanding of the meaning and significance of a service of worship before he can appreciate the importance of the way in which he performs his job. The finance committee should see its job as more than raising money, or else its methodology may be far from Christian. A teacher who is professionally competent may be ineffective as a church-school worker if his understanding of the Christian faith is inadequate. The method of the teacher must always be seen in relation to the ends in view: leading to encounter with the living God and an explication of the meaning of that encounter.

There is undoubtedly a place in leadership education for the "job analysis," for coaching in the performance of a particular job, and for the giving of help in the carrying out of a special task. But it is important that the job analysis and the coaching be done within the perspective of Christian communication. An understanding of method alone may be dangerous unless it is seen as a genuine expression of the larger purposes involved in Christian teaching and in the performing of other tasks. This will mean that "methods" courses ought to be related to "content." It will mean that the best kind of training is that which involves a combination of the use of materials and the performance of a task. Laboratory experiences, both for the teacher and for other workers, are the best kind of training, so that method and material, technique and theory, practice and principle, will be made consistent.

This approach to leadership education which seeks to combine "content" and "methodology" may be seen in the example cited in the previous chapter. Here, in a single, continuous, fifteen-week class, an attempt was made to give some introduction to the Christian message and its relation to a particular age group. It is not always possible to include all areas in one effort. Where this cannot be done, other opportunities must be offered. Further, teachers of leadership classes, as well as those who work with individual leaders, must keep this relationship in mind.

Means of Leadership Education

Here, then, are four emphases in the content of leadership education. How will this preparation be implemented? What are the occasions on which this type of help can be given? Nothing that is suggested in the following paragraphs should be thought of either in a limiting or a definitive manner. The following suggestions are to be thought of only as approaches to the matter which ought to be taken in utter seriousness by a local parish.

We start *first* with what we have said in the heart of the response of the Christian community, its services of worship. The revitalizing of the services of worship of a local church should be thought of as the first step in developing more adequate leadership. Suggestions have already been made to this effect in a previous chapter.[15] A further word may be needed concerning the sermon as an opportunity within the worship service for effectively presenting the Christian gospel.

Too many sermons consist of fairly pleasant moralizing, the buoying up of the saints, or the offering of palliatives for frustrated and unconcerned churchgoers. We need a return to preaching which deals solidly, plainly, and unflinchingly with the issues of life in the light of the Christian revelation. The pulpit must call men to repentance and faith. The motivation for Christian living, in God's action in Christ, must be clearly sounded from the pulpit, and congregations must be clear concerning the demands which their faith places upon them. The note of judgment will always be accompanied by a clear note of grace. Commitment of life in its fullness must be demanded; the assurance of the gift of power in so doing must be offered.

Second, our programs of Christian nurture and teaching must be re-evaluated in the light of both the newer insights of theology and an appreciation of the Biblical message. This must be done in terms of both a theology and an educational philosophy which are sound. Suggestions for this rethinking have already been made.[16] This must be done by those who plan and write church-school materials, to be sure, but it must also be taken seriously by pastors and directors in local churches.

This will include a more adequate program of adult education, including much more than the present Sunday-school program. Any program aimed at developing leadership is likely to fail unless it is based on a total church emphasis on adult education. Indeed, the type of lay theological education described in a previous chapter must be thought of as part of a church's total strategy for leadership education. This will involve the utilization of all possible personnel for teaching, with the pastor sharing in the teaching program, probably at times other than the Sunday-school hour.

Third, the group life of the congregation must be extended and improved along the lines suggested in a previous chapter.[17] This means that the Church must be taken seriously as the Body of Christ, and Christian forgiveness must be proclaimed and practiced. The pastor or other professional leader must begin with his own opportunities in the development of responsible group participation. The manner in which he guides the governing body of the local church, the committee on education, or the finance committee is setting the pattern by which lay personnel will deal with the groups for which they have responsibility.

Fourth, already existing forms of leadership education will be continued and expanded in revised forms. These include such items as the following in the local church: training classes for teachers, personal conferences with all leaders by pastor and other professional workers, apprenticeship, observation, the use of consulting teachers in the local situation, the women's society training programs, the training of lay evangelists, the holding of schools for ushers, and similar enterprises. Beyond the local church, it includes schools sponsored by districts, cities, and larger church areas ("Schools for Christian Workers," these are sometimes called); laboratory schools; coaching conferences; lay retreats; and so on.[18]

Fifth, new forms of leadership preparation should be established on the local church level. Classes in Bible, church history, theology, worship, and Christian ethics will be made available. Such a program might be organized into a five-year program such as Elton Trueblood proposes.[19] Lay groups such as have already been proposed may come into being out of which leadership will evolve. It will not be expected that a large number of persons in a local congregation will take advantage of such opportunities. If they did so the program might become unwieldly. The leavening of the lump must begin through a small group that becomes concerned. This matter of developing educated leadership is a long-term process.

Sixth, serious consideration should be given to short-term schools for laymen held at such centers as theological seminaries, church-related colleges, assembly grounds, and other centers. These are already in existence at such centers as Parishfield, near Brighton, Michigan, and the School of the Lay Ministry at Wittenberg College, Springfield, Ohio.[20] In the summer of 1957, several Ecumenical Institutes were held throughout the nation as experiments of a similar order. In the one in which I participated—at Perkins School of Theology, Southern Methodist University, in Dallas, Texas—a sizable group of lay persons was included, along with ministers. The work included lectures by leaders of the ecumenical movement on various phases of the movement, workshops on subjects of both practical and theoretical significance, and an ecumenical fellowship which deepened as the week progressed. Sufficient interest was generated that it seems probable that similar institutes will be conducted in the future.

The expansion of this program will necessitate an all-church and an interdenominational strategy. It may mean that the support of industry, offices, and business firms must be elicited so that they will give time off for such meetings with pay. It will not be expected that large numbers of workers in local churches will attend such schools, but if one or two can do so a beginning will be made.

What I have been describing is not a simple program. Nothing short of a complete and long-range effort will meet the need for trained, informed, and committed leadership. Until a church takes its mission of providing an educated lay leadership in utter seriousness, a significant change is not likely to occur. The recruiting and training of leaders is a continuous process. This training must not be thought of as primarily one of providing techniques. Rather it must be thought of as the projection of the idea that the Church is a fellowship of those who have responded in faith to Christ and who seek ways of serving him and their fellow men.

Such efforts, let it be repeated, will not of themselves build the Christian community. They will not even assure *Christian* leadership, since such leadership comes out of commitment, not training. They may, however, become instruments through which the Spirit can work in realizing the unity both in the local church and throughout Christendom which we seek. And they may be means both by which commitment is deepened and at the some time methodology is improved.

And God has appointed in the church first apostles, second prophets, third teachers, then workers of miracles, then healers, helpers, administrators, speakers in various kinds of tongues. Are all apostles? Are all prophets? Are all teachers? Do all work miracles? Do all possess gifts of healing? Do all speak with tongues? Do all interpret? But earnestly desire the higher gifts. (I Cor. 12:28-31a.)

Do your best to present yourself to God as one approved, a workman who has no need to be ashamed, rightly handling the word of truth. (II Tim. 2:15.)

Administering the
Fellowship

FROM TIME TO TIME IN THIS STUDY, QUESTIONS RELATIVE TO THE
manner in which the temporal life of the Church is organized
and carried out have been raised. Particularly in the sections
dealing with leadership has this been the case.[1] Thus the matter of
administration has already been considered, and the present chapter
is an attempt to bring into focus both the problems and the opportunities which are encountered in the day-by-day task of guiding the
life of the local church. Although these comments are relevant to
both the paid and the voluntary staff of the church, they are especially
aimed toward those who give full time to its work. Matters pertaining
to voluntary leadership have already been taken into account.

The Problem of Administration

That administration is a problem to the ordained ministry of the
Church has been given ample documentation of late. One of the findings of the Blizzard study of the ministry, carried out under the Russell
Sage Foundation and directed by Dr. Samuel Blizzard, is that ministers
give a disproportionate amount of their time to administration when
contrasted with the time given to preparation for preaching, to teaching,
and to other ministries.[2] Similarly, the Niebuhr study of theological
education and the ministry, made possible by the Carnegie Corpora-
tion and carried out under the auspices of the American Association
of Theological Schools, concluded that the primary role of the American
minister in the twentieth century is that of "pastoral director." This
term was somewhat arbitrarily chosen by those directing the study as
one which describes the increasing amount of attention which ministers
must give to the oversight of the total program of the local church.[3]

Further evidence of the increased amount of attention which must
be given to the *business* of the church comes from the fact that many
larger churches have included a person on the paid staff whose sole
responsibility is administration, such persons almost always being

laymen. In one church of my acquaintance, this person has large responsibility in the financial program of the church, provides co-ordination for the extensive program, and carries out all details dealing with building and equipment. In another, the administrator deals primarily with the building and with details of organization, including staff, with the minister still being chief administrator. In still another, where larger responsibilities are given to the executive assistant, it was the laymen who insisted that such a person be employed in order to release the principal pastor from many administrative duties and free him to give more time to preaching and pastoral work. In none of these three instances, however, is the principal pastor completely relieved from administrative responsibilities.

This is not a new problem, of course. The book of Acts records the appointment of the first administrative officials:

Now in these days when the disciples were increasing in number, the Hellenists murmured against the Hebrews because their widows were neglected in the daily distribution. And the twelve summoned the body of the disciples and said, "It is not right that we should give up preaching the word of God to serve tables. Therefore, brethren, pick out from among you seven men of good repute, full of the Spirit and of wisdom, whom we may appoint to this duty. But we will devote ourselves to prayer and to the ministry of the word." And what they said pleased the whole multitude, and they chose Stephen, a man full of faith and of the Holy Spirit, and Philip, and Prochorus, and Nicanor, and Timon, and Parmenas, and Nicolaus, a proselyte of Antioch. These they set before the apostles, and they prayed and laid their hands upon them. (Acts 6:1-6.)

Very early, then, the Church began to take on the characteristics of an institution as it extended its ministry to the material care of the widows within its midst. In no period of its history has it been free of this necessity. Our day has elaborated and multiplied these institutional duties as new ways have been sought to extend its mission.

Indeed, as we have seen, it is probably true that the Church has seen itself too much as an institution and too little as the Body of Christ. The solution to our dilemma, however, is not to disregard the work of administration; this cannot be done. Rather, as the Niebuhr report insists, "Clear understanding of the nature and mission of the Church are prerequisite to any effective solution of the problems that present themselves." [4] Thus, what we need in our rethinking of the nature and place of administration is a clearer understanding of its theological foundations. We must see the practical matter of "serving tables" in all of its modern extensions as a means by which the Church expresses its mission as a redemptive Community rather than as an institution of moral uplift. In the process we may find, for one thing, that we have overextended our concept of the institutional life of the Church, and second, that we have taken over into the Church ways of acting which are inconsistent with its nature and mission.

In this effort to discuss the theological basis for administration, we shall look at some dangers to be avoided, and then at an approach to administration which attempts to place it in a Christian setting. No effort will be made to deal with all the practical details of administration which in themselves would comprise a sizable book.

Dangers to Be Avoided

Administration is a means of achieving a desired goal, a way of carrying out plans. It is the method employed to put an idea into action. Consider a very simple example: if our goal is to get from New York to Chicago, we must decide on a means of travel—this is our plan of reaching our goal. Having decided to travel by train, we must buy tickets, make preparations for the trip, board the train, ride for several hours, and having arrived at our destination, alight from the train. The carrying out of plans in reaching the goal is administration.

Or suppose our goal is to make possible more adequate theological education for laymen in our church. Here too we must make plans. (The manner in which this can be done will be discussed later.) Decisions must be made concerning time, length of study, textbooks, methods of teaching, and the like. Ways of informing the congregation of this opportunity are determined. As plans are made, they must be put into action. This is administration.

1. Thus, as we think about administering the Fellowship of Faith, we must avoid a key danger, the confusing of ends and methods. Methods are not ends in themselves—the performing of a particular task in the church is not the end but a means. Further, our purposes and methods must be consistent. A four-step process thus emerges: What is the nature of the Church? How do we see its mission ("purpose") in relation to its nature? What particular program will help carry out some aspect of its mission? What methods may be used to carry out this program? Since this process will be considered in greater

detail in a later section, we need only raise the questions for the moment.

Another way of stating this *first danger* is to point to the tension which always exists between the *secularization* of the Church and its *spiritualization*, between the danger of *institutionalizing* and of vague and irrelevant *theologizing*. Secularization points to the impingement of the world upon the Church; spiritualization indicates the failure of the Church to relate meaningfully to the world.

As we have said, when a great idea is institutionalized (that is, when it is implemented by form and organization), it tends to lose its freshness, its vitality, its purity, even though such a process seems inevitable. This is illustrated by what happened to the Christian message when it became institutionalized as the official religion of the Roman Empire. So long as the movement remained a minority one, struggling for its very existence, it remained relatively free of the corrupting forces of the world. When it became the official religion of the Empire, a process was begun which led it more and more toward becoming a cultural religion. Such also has been the history of many reform movements within the Church.

Those who are involved in the day-by-day matters of carrying on the work of the local church need to be aware of this tension which exists between secularization and spiritualization. Christianity in America is continually in danger of becoming so closely related to the culture of which it is a part that it ceases to be distinguishable from that culture.[5] Yet in the modern sectarian movements, it has been tempted so to withdraw from culture that it has no effective relationship with the ongoing life of which it is a part.[6] Modern cultural Christianity must be awakened from its complacency by movements like the existentialism which stems from Sören Kierkegaard; on the other hand, it must be aware of the temptation to a kind of Protestant monasticism, which so rejects the cultural factors in current expressions of the Christian faith that it risks having any effective relationship with culture at all.

To put this dilemma in another manner, the Church is faced with the temptation to borrow the wisdom of the world without transforming that wisdom to fit its own ends. This is what happened in religious education in the fifty-year period between about 1880 and 1930, when it first began to borrow from European educators and afterwards took over the theories of John Dewey. Great new things were happening in education, the Church could hardly ignore them. But in listening to them it tended to capitulate to them. Religious education often became hardly distinguishable from character education, and the distinctly Christian element was sometimes omitted.

Such is the temptation today with respect to psychotherapy. The question which faces the area of pastoral counseling is similar to that which faced religious education fifty years ago. Will pastoral counseling tend to become either a slightly Christianized version of secular psychotherapy or a secularized version of pastoral care, or can it escape the snare in which the Church is continually in danger of being caught as it faces the culture of which it is a part? [7] This same danger is being faced in the area of "group dynamics," with the result that sometimes church meetings appear to be more "group-conscious" than "Christ-conscious."

So it is with the realm of program-planning and administration. Niebuhr has stated this danger so well that it seems appropriate to quote several sentences:

A second indirect indication of the character of the new conception of the ministry may be gained from a glance at its perverse form—the one in which the pastoral director becomes the "big operator." When ministers comment on the kinds of men who are failures in the ministry they frequently describe among these types the person who operates a religious club or a neighborhood society with much efficiency and pomp and circumstance. He is active in many affairs, organizes many societies, advertises the increases in membership and budget achieved under his administration and, in general, manages church business as if it were akin to the activities of a chamber of commerce. In their reaction to such secularization of the office some men try to return to the idea of the preacher or of the priest. But the needs of men and the responsibilities of office prevent them from doing so. Then they realize that the "big operator" represents a perversion of the minister's office not because he is an executive but because he does not administer the *church's* work. [8]

The danger, then, is that the minister will borrow from the world the concept of the executive and fail to baptize this concept with the more inclusive one of the nature of the Church as the Body of Christ.

In matters of finance, in carrying on its business affairs, in planning its buildings, and even in teaching, counseling, and preaching, the minister must try to avoid both the extreme of adapting these to the ways of the world and that of failing to relate them in any meaningful manner to the culture of which he is a part.

2. The *second* of these sets of dangers in program-planning and administration places in tension the *activism* which often characterizes the American Church and the *passivism* of which the European Church is often guilty. On the one hand, this is the temptation to become so involved in an active church program that one seems by implication to be seeking to build God's kingdom by his own efforts, while on the other, to place so little importance on man's effort that preaching and the administration of the Sacraments become the only means by which the organized church expresses itself in the world.

With this in mind every local church in America ought to evaluate its program in terms of the demands which it makes upon its constituents, its tendency to take parents out of the home for a multitude of activities, its temptation to conceive its youth program in terms of "keeping them busy." Perhaps it is doing some things that are not really necessary; perhaps it is doing others for the wrong reason (for example, what is the motive behind the church's recreational program for young people?); perhaps there are areas of church life which are neglected. The central criterion for evaluation must be whether a particular part of the program is preparing the soil for the receiving of the Spirit of God.

On the other hand, some churches may not be active enough! Although this passivism is often associated with European Christianity, it is also characteristic of a fair number of American churches. Many local churches do not place enough emphasis on proportionate giving, on an active program for young people, on social evils existent in the community. This statement is borne out by the large number of student pastors in seminary whose lament is that they are unable to wake up their congregations, to get them moving. Indeed, the seemingly excessive number of "directives" which come to the local church from higher headquarters of the church is partly, if not largely, due to the failure of local churches to assume their own responsibilities.

Whatever the tendency of the particular church, however, the motivation for acting must come out of the congregation's understanding of who it is. The place to begin, as we have said and will say more fully in the next section, is with the Church as the Body of Christ in the world.

3. The *third* set of dangers concerns the tension between what may

157

be called *"blueprintism"* and *structurelessness*. The former, which is the temptation of many churchmen, leads to the acceptance uncritically of someone else's plans, perhaps those handed on from higher headquarters. The education staff of the conference, synod, or convention suggests, let us say, that promotion Sunday ought to be the last Sunday in September; so without any question as to whether this is the best thing for a particular situation, the local church follows the plan. Church "A" has worked out an effective means of providing family-life education for its parents, so Church "B" adopts the plan without particular modification for its own needs. The follower of this approach (and there are both clergymen and laymen involved) avidly attends meetings, reads books, scans periodicals, visits other churches in his search for a blueprint he can follow in his own parish. When he attends a meeting or reads a book on the work of the local church and does not come away with a plan he can put to work, he feels his time has been wasted.

Now it is quite possible for one person to present to another the plans for building a table, or making a dress, or laying a patio. Any enterprise involving *things* primarily may be done according to a blueprint. So long as the relationship in an undertaking is primarily an "I-it" relationship, it is comparatively easy to follow a set of plans. But the moment an undertaking involves *persons*, the situation changes. Things ("it's") remain relatively constant and predictable; persons are individuals who change, who are affected by relationships in a way that things are not. A plan which works with one group may simply not work with another.

But there is another side to the matter involving even greater dangers. When an enterprise involving persons is carried out with the idea that it can be done according to a set of plans either worked out in another situation or even prepared in advance for that particular setting, the persons involved are then treated as things rather than persons. Whenever the people involved are not given priority over plans, whenever any plan is thought of as a blueprint to be followed, then the persons are really being treated as things to be manipulated into place, not persons to be related to. Persons, under such administration, are being used for the ends of the administrator, or leader, even when the leader thinks he is doing this for their own good. Whenever a leader seeks to get people to some preconceived end (which is what a blueprint calls for), he is trespassing on their freedom. Even God does not do this. All of this may be summarized in the statement: *things are to be used and manipulated, persons are to be related to.*

But the opposite extreme of this danger is also to be avoided. This may be called the danger of *structurelessness,* or waiting for something to happen. What has been said by way of criticism of programs handed down from higher headquarters is not meant to imply that there is no value in such planning. Nor is this meant to imply that we do not learn from reading about, observing, and participating in what other groups have done. A person who faces his task of leadership void of any ideas concerning what has been done in similar situations is acting as if he were not in the company of a great cloud of witnesses. An administrator who has not carefully thought through the problem to be considered in a committee meeting is not likely to be a helpful leader of that committee.

Somehow, then, we must avoid both "blueprintism" and structure-lessness.

4. A *fourth* set of dangers concerns the manner in which the local church deals with changing circumstances. On one side is *the danger of being unwilling to make changes in the structures from the past,* while on the other is the opposite *danger of refusing to accept the structures from the past at all.*

How many things are done in local churches or on a national level just because they happen to have been done that way in the past! Structures in which we operate can easily become sacred; they may even become the gods that stand between us and the God and Father of our Lord Jesus Christ. What local church has not refused to make a change on no other basis than that "it has always been done this way"? Here is a church which has been in a rural area, carrying out its mission reasonably well through church services, Sunday school, and the midweek prayer meeting. When it finds itself in the midst of a new suburban development, the question is whether it responds to a set of changed conditions with a program that fits these new conditions. In one such church which refused to move with the times, new residents insisted upon the establishing of a new church. Had the older church met the challenge of changed circumstances, this move could have been avoided until the situation demanded another church.

This question is an especially crucial one in our time when such rapid changes are taking place in all areas of life, but especially in urban areas. Churches in the so-called "fringe" sections (those changing from residential to apartment or semibusiness districts, or those in which the constituency of the neighborhood is being altered) particularly face the necessity of modifying their programs. This matter is being met far too inadequately by the churches involved.[9]

As we have indicated, however, the opposite extreme is also a danger: namely, the kind of fear of the past which means that it is essentially and effectively ignored. A pastor who goes into a new church and begins a revolution is guilty of this sin. A critic of the modern church who sees its ineffectiveness and then demands a clean sweep of all its structure is in the same category. The function of history is to illuminate the present; so it is with the organizational and program structures of the past. Neither demands slavery to the past, nor does the present, even in our rapid period of transition, demand a sweeping away of all that has been.

In our implementing of the Christian faith, let us neither be wedded to the structures of the past nor unmindful of their existence.

In the total matter of program-planning and administration, then, we must be careful to keep our understanding of the Church foremost; to act, but always in harmony with this basic insight; to use the structures provided by the common experience of the total organized church as guides, not as blueprints; and to utilize the insights of the past for edification in our particular setting.

A Christian View of Administration

Keeping in mind these dangers inherent in the Church's attempt to implement its message in the world, let us now turn to a Christian view of administration. Administration is, as we have said, nothing more than a way of getting things done, of accomplishing some end. It is a means of bridging the gap between idea and action, between principle and practice. Christian administration, then, is a way of ordering the life of the local church (or of any other level of the life of the Church) so that it is prepared to receive the gift of God's Spirit and so radiate into the larger community as to make known that Spirit outside its own boundaries. A program is not something to "put over," or even to "put on"; a church is not something to be "run" like a locomotive. Rather a program is a structure, partly determined by outside forces, partly determined by a local fellowship, always determined by the nature of the Church itself, through which the living God *may* be made known to human persons. Administering the

160

Fellowship is the guiding of the Fellowship in the developing of its own interior life and the helping of it to find means of manifesting its life in the larger community.

In other words, administration is not something done simply to carry on the institutional life of the Church, or for that matter of any agency. When it becomes this, then the agency, be it Church or other, is simply perpetuating itself. Rather administration is a process for making possible the carrying out of certain ends—purposes not exterior to the life of the agency (such as the Church), but those inherent within the nature of the agency itself (or so far as the Church is concerned in the Christian gospel).

There is therefore nothing sacrosanct about existing structures nor even about the institutional life of the Church. Such structures must be continually re-examined. If means out of harmony with the basic structure of the gospel must be used in order to raise the money to build a new church building, then the church must re-examine its purposes of building a new building. If the getting of members is simply *the getting of members for the sake of keeping up denominational statistics,* and if in such "evangelism" persons are brought into the Fellowship without evidence of commitment or without preparation for membership, then both end and means must be re-evaluated. Until ends and means are consonant with the nature of the gospel of God, then both must be called into question.

With this background in mind, let us now look at some "practical" aspects of the life of the local fellowship. The following suggestions should not be thought of exactly as "steps," though there is some logic in the order in which they are set forth. Certainly they should not be thought of as a blueprint, but rather as a kind of structure within which administration can take place.

As a point of departure in considering the nature of Christian administration, we begin with that experience from which the Christian faith derives: *the encounter of man with God.* This is the experience described in both the Old and New Testaments; that is the historic Church; and that of the living Church today—local, national, world. In other words we begin with God's action. This is symbolized in the doctrine of the Trinity: God as Creator, God as Redeemer, God as Sustainer. It is focused in the Word made flesh—the incarnation in which God most dramatically made himself known to man. The message of the incarnation finds current meaning through the continuing activity of God through the Holy Spirit. The place to begin in thinking about administration is the relationship of man and Church with God, historically expressed and currently known.

Closely related to the encounter itself is *the theologizing about the encounter as it occurred in Jesus Christ and as it occurs today*. This has led to a body of doctrines which are not the gospel though they do point us to the gospel. Among them are certain ideas about the nature of the Church, these concepts having arisen in the process by which the Church has expressed itself in the world for nineteen centuries.

The means of expression which have arisen include worship as the central response of the Church. Other modes are found in the offices of preaching, teaching, pastoral care, and outreach (evangelism, missions, service, social action). These major offices have remained relatively constant in the history of the Christian community, though their precise meaning, significance, and relationship to one another have been continually re-evaluated. For example, we are now witnessing a resurgence of emphasis on the pastoral office through the impact of psychotherapy. It may be that we need to reassert the teaching function because of the tendency of the historic memory of the Church to be obscured or unknown even in the experience of active church people today.

Further, more exact formulations of how these purposes are to be expressed must be related to concrete situations. The exact manner in which the teaching ministry is to be performed will vary from local church to local church. It may be that some structure other than the Sunday school as it has developed during the past century ought to be formulated. The content of the teaching program will vary also. In some churches the approach to using the Bible may be the breaking down of the idolatrous notion concerning the sacredness of the words of the Bible themselves, whereas in others one must begin with the assumption that the Bible is virtually ignored by the people. The particular way in which each local church carries out its mission will be conditioned by the community in which it is set. Many factors must be taken into account as program is formulated.

This rethinking must be done partly by those engaged in the higher echelons of church administration. Theological seminaries are one of the modern centers for this rethinking, the faculties of these institutions being responsible for being in the vanguard of such theologizing. Church boards and agencies must lead the Church into new areas

162

of thought, into fresh expressions of the Christian faith, into pioneer efforts to communicate the gospel today. Particular responsibility is laid upon those in charge of the planning, editing, and writing of church-school lesson materials since the content of the teaching of most local churches is considerably influenced by what goes into lesson materials.

This process of rethinking must also take place on the local level. The responsibility for leading such a process must rest heavily upon the minister (and his staff if he is in a church large enough to employ such a staff). Too little of this process actually goes on in most local churches. Often a minister arrives at a local church with a set of presuppositions. If he is vigorous in his leadership and if he inspires his people to follow him, his program may be "put over." If he tends to take the path of least resistance or if he meets with opposition, he may be tempted to do nothing. Rather he ought to lead the parish members in a re-examination of who they are, what the Church is, what its message is, and what its business is.

The place to begin in considering administration, then, is with the nature of the encounter between God and man, the faith which results, and the Church which has come into being.

An Approach to Procedure

1. *The first step in procedure is to know the Church and its faith.*
2. *The second is to know the situation and its people.*

Whoever the leader is (minister, director of Christian education, or lay leader), he must know a situation and the people involved before the work of planning is begun. He observes, listens, asks questions, comes to know people, evaluates. As he comes to know the situation and the people, he will look for potentialities as well as weaknesses. He will begin to sense areas where action may be possible. Then as he assumes his role of active leadership he will come to it with some understanding of what is needed and how best to proceed.

3. *Having prepared himself, it is now time to involve the people.*

Let us assume for the moment that the administrator is the pastor of a small church. In such a case it may be possible to involve the entire congregation in a parish workshop that begins with step (1) above, moves to step (2), and then begins to formulate plans in accordance with the needs of the situation. On the basis of this study, the program emphases will be formulated.

163

Most likely it would be discovered that three levels of effort would be needed in the process of working out program emphases.

a) Some phases of the work of the local fellowship could be carried on essentially as constituted without major change.

b) Other activities now being carried out might need to be dropped, while others would necessitate major changes.

c) Still others would need to be initiated where nothing was being done. Let us say that it is discovered that the church is doing almost nothing in helping parents in the nurture of their children, and further that there are few family-centered activities being carried out. One of the program emphases might then be attempts to strengthen family life and to make the church more family centered. Perhaps it is discovered that the young people feel a need for a more thorough study of the Bible. This might lead to the development of a special year's emphasis on Bible content study.

In larger churches a different approach would be needed. Since the entire congregation or even a sizable portion of it could not participate in an all-parish planning session, subgroups would have to do the work. In this case either the existing governing body or some specially appointed group would need first to consider the matter, and later involve all the constituent groups, such as church school classes, commissions, committees, youth groups, study groups, women's groups, and the like. Such groups, having considered not only their particular interests but also the entire mission and program of the Church, would then report back to the over-all planning agency, who would co-ordinate and correlate the separate reports. From this study the general lines of advance would be set forth. Such a process involves time and patient effort, but would seem to be sound from a Christian perspective and might well mean a revival of the total life of the congregation.

Where churches are not ready for such a complete restudy, the minister may need to choose areas of action for such planning. For example, such a decision might entail a study of how the church is touching the lives of parents, and the program changes involve this area only. Such a study might be the beginning of a complete self-study by the entire church.

4. *After program emphases have been decided, then organization is necessary for the specific planning of program and for carrying it out.*

Here the committee structure of the congregation must be examined to determine what groups already in existence can be responsible for some areas, which new ones must be established, and which old ones can be discarded. If the plan is an all-church one, then the alloting of responsibility and the correlation of plans would need to be carefully worked out, with some member of the staff serving as co-ordinator.

The committees should be sufficiently large to be representative but not too large to be unwieldly. Their work would consist of the actual planning and administering of all or part of the program in question. The process of committee action is something like this:

the making of plans by the entire group
the alloting of responsibility
checking by the chairman to see how much progress is being made
reports back to the committee by responsible individuals or sub-
  committees at regular intervals
correlation of plans and the further allotment of responsibility
the completion of plans
the beginning of the program
evaluation and continued planning

5. *This process of rethinking must be a continuous one.*

If a long-range plan is adopted (let us say a five-year plan), then it must not be thought of as a rigid structure to be followed slavishly, but only as a guide line for the future. There is no end to such program-planning if the congregation is to remain dynamic.

The Role of the Professional Leader

The type of administration suggested above involves the largest number of persons possible in both policy-making and the carrying out of policy. It is a serious effort to implement the principle of the priesthood of believers, the Church as the *koinonia*. It takes seriously the idea of the Church as the corporate Body of Christ, with individuality of function by separate members.

Does this mean, then, that the professional leader, either clergyman or director of Christian education, has no significant role in the process? This question does not involve the role of the ordained minister as preacher, in conducting the services of worship, in administering the Sacraments, and in performing other roles clearly priestly in character. Rather it concerns his administrative role. Is there room for the professional worker in the administration of a church or should this be left entirely to laymen?

That there *is* a place for the professional worker has been implied at various places in the discussion of the process. Often, for example, it is the staff worker who must initiate the process. His specialized training should provide him with the understanding, insight, information, and skills which others in the congregation do not have. His role is to be initiator of the *process*, however, *not* initiator of the *plan*.

Further, he must do considerable work "behind the scenes." This involves personal conferences with the lay leadership involved in the process. He may need to enlist the interest of persons not already concerned. He will probably need to act as co-ordinator of the entire process. His motive ought not to be to convince these leaders that they must follow his ideas, but rather to work with them in the development of their ideas. Sometimes he will need to help them understand the democratic process of conducting meetings.

Much detail work (such as writing letters, sending out notices, mimeographing, co-ordinating reports, and similar tasks) will have to be done by whatever professional secretarial staff is available. If there is none, then a volunteer corps of such workers must be recruited.

Whatever professional staff the church possesses, then, will be available in the work of administration for whatever is to be done. They will not hesitate to suggest, guide, encourage, perhaps even prod. Though they may have certain ends in mind and will not hesitate at the proper time to let these be known, they will not seek to trick persons into seeking their suggestions.

Two objections will be raised immediately to this type of administration. For one thing, it is a slow process. To be sure it is, and one must have a conviction that the process is important as well as the ends sought or he is not likely to follow it. He must recognize that Christian *koinonia* is not so much an end to be sought as something which develops through relationships. This involves an approach to the Church which considers it not primarily as an institution to be promoted but as a fellowship to be lived. The living of the fellowship through such a process as has been described will then be considered as important as the actual achievement of the program ends.

The second objection will be to the effect that the results will not always be what is desired. To this we raise the question: desired by whom? If the ends set up through democratic planning are less than

Christian, then the first responsibility of the minister in working with his people becomes that of confronting them with a more adequate understanding of the gospel. Nor is it necessarily true that laymen, when led to think seriously and prayerfully about the message and mission of the Church, will not reach toward ends which are Christian. There are many risks involved in the process, of course, and it must be said again that a person must believe that the process itself is important if he is to follow this procedure.

Toward the Achievement of Koinonia

What we have said in the preceding paragraphs is that the membership of a local church ought to be led to think seriously about the message and mission of the Church and to plan the work of the local fellowship in the light of the deeper understanding achieved. This is not offered as a panacea for all the ills that beset the modern church. It is not suggested as an automatic way by which Christian *koinonia* will be achieved. This is a gift of God and cannot be manipulated into being. But the soil can be prepared and the watering can be done so that persons may be prepared to receive the gift of God's Spirit.

We have placed great emphasis upon the Church as a corporate body, believing that this is true to the New Testament conception of the Church. We have also insisted that in the final analysis it is the individual who is called of God, it is he who stands before God, it is he who must relate personally to God. To be sure he lives in fellowship, and he must experience some degree of fellowship in order to respond personally. But it is he alone who must accept responsibility for himself. In the accepting of responsibility, he becomes a free man.

For none of these aspects of the life of the Church can there be a blueprint to follow, a set of steps which can be pursued with guaranteed results. To attempt such a plan is to make "things" out of the persons who compose the fellowship.

This much can be said, however: the congregation that is aware of its mission, that is alert to its task, that is responsive to God's call, is in a position to receive the Spirit of God. What has been written in preceding pages is an attempt to call those who read to respond, in the hope that they in turn will call others to a similar response. If even a few members of a local fellowship accept their mission in utter seriousness, the interior life of that fellowship will be enriched and its influence in the world will be increased.

If the Church is to be the Church of Jesus Christ, it must see itself as his Body, his Community, his People. We cannot use God to serve *our* purposes; we can allow him to use *us* to serve *his*. His purposes can be realized through us. His work can be done through us. His gifts bring with them the necessity of our response. Our acceptance of that responsibility assures us of the gift of power. Life's meaning is found as our lives are centered in him.

What then is Apollos? What is Paul? Servants through whom you believed, as the Lord assigned to each. I planted, Apollos watered, but God gave the growth. So neither he who plants nor he who waters is anything, but only God who gives the growth. He who plants and he who waters are equal, and each shall receive his wages according to his labor. For we are fellow workmen for God; you are God's field, God's building. (I Cor. 3:5-9.)

Notes

CHAPTER I

1. See, for example, the volume prepared for the First Assembly of the World Council of Churches, *Man's Disorder and God's Design* (New York: Harper & Bros., 1949), and the similar volume prepared for the Second Assembly, *The Christian Hope and the Task of the Church* (New York: Harper & Bros., 1954). The volume edited by R. Newton Flew, *The Nature of the Church* (New York: Harper & Bros., 1952) consists of various statements presented to the Theological Commission appointed by the Continuation Committee of the World Conference on Faith and Order.
2. For a preliminary report on the Blizzard study, see Samuel W. Blizzard, "The Minister's Dilemma," *The Christian Century*, LXXIII, No. 17 (April 25, 1956), 508-10.
3. Cf. Richard Niebuhr, in collaboration with Daniel Day Williams and James M. Gustafson, *The Purpose of the Church and Its Ministry* (New York: Harper & Bros., 1956). That this is not the only dimension of the Niebuhr study is indicated not only in the first volume but also in the second which has been issued, *The Ministry in Historical Perspectives*, ed. Richard Niebuhr and Daniel Day Williams (New York: Harper & Bros., 1956).
4. "Urgent Problems of Laymen's Work: Some Conclusions," in Papers of the Ecumenical Institute, No. iii, *Professional Life as Christian Vocation: A Report on Laymen's Institutes and Groups*, 1947-48 (Geneva: Oikumene), p. 72. Used by permission of the World Council of Churches.

CHAPTER II

1. From *The Structure of the Divine Society*, by F. W. Dillistone. 1951, The Westminster Press. Pp. 154-68.
2. *Ibid.*, pp. 160-61.
3. Cf. Wilhelm Pauck, "The Ministry in the Time of the Continental Reformation," *The Ministry in Historical Perspectives*, ed. H. Richard Niebuhr and Daniel D. Williams (New York: Harper & Bros., 1956), pp. 110 ff.; and Sidney E. Mead, "The Rise of the Evangelical Conception of the Ministry in America (1607-1850)" in *ibid.*, pp. 207 ff.
4. On this latter point, see Mead, *ibid.*, pp. 214-15.

5. Quoted in Dillistone, *op. cit.*, p. 166.
6. Some of the smaller sects, it is true, have remained almost completely congregational, as has at least one fairly large and rapidly growing group, the Church of Christ. This group, an offshoot from the Disciples of Christ, has no official publication, any local church being able to begin the publication of church-school materials, which may then be used by other local churches. For all practical purposes each local church is separate and distinct from other such churches.
7. See John Donne, "The Tolling Bell—A Devotion."
8. For perhaps the best psychological discussion of the nature of selfhood, see Gardner Murphy, *Personality: A Biosocial Approach to Origin and Structure* (New York: Harper & Bros., 1947); also Gordon Allport, *Becoming: Basic Considerations for a Psychology of Personality* (New Haven: Yale University Press, 1955). For a theological discussion of the self see Reinhold Niebuhr, *The Self and the Dramas of History* (New York: Charles Scribner's Sons, 1955). For a classic discussion of this matter, see Martin Buber, *I and Thou*, tr. Ronald Gregor Smith (Edinburgh: T. & T. Clark, 1937).
9. *Man's Need and God's Action* (Greenwich, Conn.: The Seabury Press, 1953).
10. See also Col. 1:18, 24, and I Cor. 10:16-17.
11. See Dillistone, *op. cit.*, especially Sec. iii.
12. For a simple but profound discussion of this, see Reuel Howe, *op. cit.*, pp. 53-61. For a more extensive discussion, see Oscar Cullman, *Baptism in the New Testament* (Chicago: Henry Regnery Co., 1950); and P. T. Forsyth, *Lectures on the Church and the Sacraments* (London: Longmans, Green & Co., 1917), chs. ix-xi.
13. With our greater understanding of the growth and development of the human self—with its various levels of understanding, responsibility, and "accountability"—it seems logical that we must revise our understanding of both when and how a child reaches the "age of accountability." A preschool child may be considered responsible in certain areas of his life, and thus accountable to God, while it may be adolescence before a person is capable of the commitment of the entire self to God.
14. From "The Order for Receiving Persons into the Church," *Doctrines and Discipline of The Methodist Church*, 1956 (Nashville: The Methodist Publishing House, 1952), p. 554.
15. From *The Structure of the Divine Society*, by F. W. Dillistone. 1951, The Westminster Press. P. 222. See also pp. 221-22.
16. *Ibid.*, p. 232.
17. Quoted in *ibid.*, p. 233, from *Journal of Theological Studies*, XLIX, 200-201.
18. From *The Misunderstanding of the Church*, by Emil Brunner. Copyright 1953, W. L. Jenkins, The Westminster Press. Pp. 11-12.
19. From the ritual for reception of members into The Methodist Church.
20. From Article of Religion XIII of The Methodist Church, found in *Doctrines and Discipline of The Methodist Church*, 1952, p. 28.
21. From John Wesley's description of the early Methodist societies, still in the General Rules of The Methodist Church, and found in *ibid.*, p. 35.

CHAPTER III

1. From *The Significance of the Church,* by Robert McAfee Brown. Copyright 1954, W. L. Jenkins, The Westminster Press. P. 34.

2. *Loc. cit.* The Housman poem is from *The Collected Poems of A. E. Housman* and is used by permission of Henry Holt & Co.

3. For a presentation of this idea, see Randolph C. Miller, *Biblical Theology and Christian Education* (New York: Charles Scribner's Sons, 1956), especially Ch. II. See also Bernhard Anderson, *Rediscovering the Bible* (New York: Association Press, 1951).

4. *The Old Testament Against Its Environment* (Chicago: Henry Regnery Co., 1950), p. 49. Used by permission of the publisher.

5. William Barclay, *A New Testament Wordbook* (Chicago: Student Christian Movement Book Club, 1955), p. 35. Used by permission of S.C.M. Press and Harper & Bros.

6. *Loc. cit.*

7. *Unitive Protestantism: A Story of Our Religious Resources* (New York: The Abingdon Press, 1930), p. 38.

8. *Ibid.,* p. 36.

9. *Loc. cit.*

10. Quoted by E. Wolf, in *The Ministry and the Sacraments* (Report of the Theological Commission appointed by the Continuation Committee of the Faith and Order Movement under the chairmanship of the Right Rev. Arthur Cayley Headlam, ed. Roderic Dunkerley) (New York: The Macmillan Company, 1937), p. 440. Quoted from Luther, *Works,* Erlanger Edition, XL, 171.

11. *The Misunderstanding of the Church* (Philadelphia: The Westminster Press, 1953), Ch. iii.

12. For further discussion of this point, see Herbert H. Farmer, "The Bible: Its Significance and Authority," *The Interpreter's Bible,* I (Nashville: Abingdon Press, 1952), 3-31.

13. I have documented this history in an unpublished dissertation on file at Columbia University, *Making Lay Leadership Effective: A Historical Study of Major Issues in the Use of Laymen by The Methodist Church Especially for Its Educational Program* (New York: Columbia University, 1949).

14. For documentation of this movement, see *ibid.*

15. Cf. Clarence P. Shedd, *Two Centuries of Student Christian Movements* (New York: Association Press, 1934), Ch. i.

16. Grimes, *op. cit.,* pp. 34-35.

17. *Ibid.,* pp. 35-37.

18. *Ibid.,* pp. 37-38.

19. First Assembly of the World Council of Churches, Amsterdam, 1948, *Memoranda on Concerns of the Churches:* . . . "The Training of Laymen in the Church". . . (Geneva: World Council of Churches, Route de Malagnou 17), pp. 15-16. Used by permission of the World Council of Churches.

20. "The Laity—The Christian in His Vocation" (Part VI of the volume prepared for use by the Second Assembly of the World Council of Churches, 1954,

and called *The Christian Hope and the Task of the Church* [New York: Harper & Bros., 1954]), p. 1. Used by permission.
21. *Infra*, Chap. VIII.

CHAPTER IV

1. Cf. Harry C. Munro, *Protestant Nurture* (New York: Prentice-Hall, Inc., 1956), pp. 153-54.
2. *The Misunderstanding of the Church* (Philadelphia: The Westminster Press, 1953), p. 12.
3. *Ibid.*, p. 118.
4. *The Realm of Redemption: Studies in the Doctrine of the Nature of the Church in Contemporary Protestant Theology* (Greenwich, Conn.: The Seabury Press, 1951), pp. 103-4. Used by permission of publisher.
5. See James A. Peterson, *Education for Marriage* (New York: Charles Scribner's Sons, 1956), especially Part iv.
6. What is said here concerning group feeling is amplified considerably in Chap. VIII, which considers the nature of group life according to modern experimentation and study.
7. J. Y. Campbell, "KOINONIA and Its Cognates in the New Testament," *Journal of Biblical Literature*, LI (1932), 353.
8. *Ibid.*, p. 356.
9. *The Common Life in the Body of Christ* (Westminster: Dacre Press: A.&C. Black, 1941), p. 31. The complete quotation from Vincent is as follows: Koinonia refers to "a relation between individuals which involves common and mutual interest and participation in a common object." (*A Critical and Exegetical Commentary on the Epistles to the Philippians and to Philemon* [New York: Charles Scribner's Sons, 1911], pp. 6-7.)
10. *Ibid.*, p. 16.
11. *Ibid.*, p. 327.
12. Quoted from Campbell, *op. cit.*, p. 353.
13. Reference is here made to C. H. Dodd's *The Johannine Epistles*, pp. 6 f.
14. Nelson, *op. cit.*, p. 53. Used by permission of Seabury Press.
15. Chap. II.
16. *Letters to Young Churches: A Translation of the New Testament Epistles* (New York: The Macmillan Company, 1955), p. 117. Used by permission of the publisher.
17. It would appear wrong to interpret these two passages as reflecting an economic system which has sometimes been called "primitive communism." It is doubtful if the early Christians had any such idea. Rather the holding of things in common was a natural outgrowth of the close fellowship which characterized the early church, along with their expectation of the early return of Christ.
18. *Man's Need and God's Action* (Greenwich, Conn.: The Seabury Press, 1953), p. 56 and *passim*. See also Paul Tillich, *The Courage to Be* (New Haven: Yale University Press, 1952), pp. 163-67 and *passim*.
19. Tillich, *op. cit.*, pp. 46-51, 57-63, and *passim*; Rollo May, *Man's Search for Himself* (New York: W. W. Norton & Co., 1953), chs. i and ii.

CHAPTER V

1. Cf. Alan Richardson, *The Biblical Doctrine of Work: Ecumenical Biblical Studies No. 1* (London: Student Christian Movement Press, 1952); Paul S. Minear, "Work and Vocation in Scripture," in *Work and Vocation: A Christian Discussion,* ed. John Oliver Nelson (New York: Harper & Bros., 1954), ch. i.

2. *Ibid.,* p. 71. Used by permission of Harper & Bros.

3. *Op cit.,* p. 37. Used by permission of S.C.M. Press.

4. "Work and Vocation in Christian History," in *Work and Vocation: A Christian Discussion,* p. 99 and entire chapter.

5. *Ibid.,* p. 108.

6. Current thinking concerning a special call to Church service is divided. Minear discusses briefly the fact that the New Testament indicates that such special calls do exist, as in I Cor. 12:4-11, Rom. 13:3-8, and Eph. 4:11-12. (*Op. cit.,* p. 66.) It is significant, of course, that in each case the special call is the result of special gifts. Richardson, on the other hand, specifically states that there is *no* difference in the call to the Church's professional ministry and the call to its other ministries. "The New Testament doctrine of vocation does not countenance the view that one may be called to the Church as a profession! It is rather that, having received the call to the ministry (which every member of the *Laos,* or laymen, receives), the ordained, with the consent and authorization of the Church, resolves to exercise his gift of ministry in the particular office of the regular ministry of the Word and Sacraments, believing that this is the will of Christ for him." (*Op. cit.,* p. 37.) It would appear that his last phrase, "the will of Christ for him," does approach very nearly the idea of a specific call. It is true, however, that evangelical Protestantism would have saved itself many unhappy experiences with its ordained ministry had it been more careful in carrying out the Biblical requirement for validating a special call (if such exists), namely, special gifts which fit one for the work of the ordained ministry. Similarly, some might enter the ordained ministry who do not now do so were it not for the expectation of this special call.

7. For a documentation of this struggle, see Henry F. May, *Protestant Churches and Industrial America* (New York: Harper & Bros., 1949).

8. Published by the Lutterworth Press (London, 1951).

9. Published as part of the omnibus volume prepared for the 1954 Assembly of the World Council of Churches, *The Christian Hope and the Task of the Church* (New York: Harper & Bros., 1954), Part iv.

10. Edited by and with an introduction by John Oliver Nelson (New York: Harper & Bros., 1954).

11. Chap. III.

12. "The Laity—The Christian in His Vocation," in *The Christian Hope and the Task of the Church,* p. 1. Used by permission of Harper & Bros.

13. *Ibid.,* pp. 49-50.

14. Paul Quillian, *Not a Sparrow Falls* (Nashville: Abingdon Press, 1952), p. 27. See also the sermon entitled "The Preachers in the Pews."

THE CHURCH REDEMPTIVE

15. Richard Niebuhr, *The Purpose of the Church and Its Ministry* (New York: Harper & Bros., 1956), pp. 21-22.
16. Cf. Robert S. Michaelsen, "Work and Vocation in American Industrial Society," in *Work and Vocation: A Christian Discussion*, ch. iii.

CHAPTER VI

1. Article of Religion XIII, The Methodist Church. A similar statement is used by many of the major Protestant groups as a definition of the Church.
2. The hero of Leigh Hunt's poem by the same name.
3. From John Milton's sonnet, "On His Blindness."
4. This paraphrase was suggested to me by Professor Fred Gealy of the Perkins School of Theology faculty. It should be noted that the modifying adjective, *logikos*, is just as difficult to render, as is illustrated by the varying translations, "reasonable," "spiritual," and "rational." This is not our concern here, however.
5. From the exegesis of "Romans," in *The Interpreter's Bible* (Nashville: Abingdon Press, 1954), IX, 581.
6. Cf. George Hedley, *Christian Worship* (New York: The Macmillan Company, 1953), pp. 1-2.
7. William Barclay, *A New Testament Wordbook* (Chicago: Student Christian Movement Book Club, 1955), pp. 75-76.
8. *The Shape of the Liturgy* (Westminster: Dacre Press, 1945), especially Chs. i and ii. See also Barclay, *op. cit.*, pp. 74-76.
9. *The Eucharistic Hymns of John and Charles Wesley* (London: The Epworth Press, 1948), pp. 154-55. Used by permission of the publisher.
10. *The Religious Consciousness* (New York: The Macmillan Company, 1920), especially Ch. xiv.
11. As Richard Niebuhr has pointed out, "The objection that God is never object but always subject often arises from a confusion of the word 'object' as meaning 'thing' with 'object' as meaning the Other toward which sensation, thought, appreciation, worship, et cetera are directed." (*The Purpose of the Church and Its Ministry* [New York: Harper & Bros., 1956], p. 19, n. 6.) Used by permission.
12. July 25, 1955. As reported in *Time*, LXVI, No. 6 (August 8, 1955), 62. Used by permission.
13. *Vital Elements of Public Worship* (London: The Epworth Press, 1936, 3rd ed., 1954), p. 9. Used by permission of the publisher.
14. As reported in a communication called "Study Religion's Role in Culture," *The Christian Century*, LXXI (January 20, 1954), 95.
15. Cf. A. G. Hebert, *Liturgy and Society* (London: Faber and Faber, Ltd., 1935), pp. 125-38.
16. *We Shall Re-Build: The Work of Iona Community on Mainland and on Island* (Glasgow: The Iona Community [n.d.,]), p. 33.
17. Edited by G. Ernest Osborn and published by the Christian Board of Publications, St. Louis, 1953.
18. For further discussion of the elements of a worship serivce, see Massey

174

Shepherd, *The Worship of the Church* (Greenwich, Conn.: The Seabury Press, 1952), Ch. ii.

19. *The Book of Worship for Church and Home* (Nashville: The Methodist Publishing House, 1944).

20. The Rev. Terry Thomason, of the Oklahoma Conference, now in the Boston University School of Theology.

21. See his essay, "Demythologizing the Gospel," in *Kerygma and Myth*, ed. Hans Werner Bartsch, tr. Reginald H. Fuller (London: Society for the Promotion of Christian Knowledge, 1953).

22. *Dogmatics in Outline* (New York: Philosophical Library, 1949), pp. 30-34.

23. For additional suggestions, see Raymond E. Balcomb, "Creative Revival of Worship," *The Pastor*, XVIII, No. 1 (January, 1955), 26-28.

24. *A Historical Approach to Evangelical Worship* (Nashville: Abingdon Press, 1954), especially p. 287.

25. See John Knox, *The Integrity of Preaching* (Nashville: Abingdon Press, 1957).

26. Chap. II.

27. Cf. J. Ernest Rattenbury, *The Eucharistic Hymns of John and Charles Wesley*, pp. 4-5. This interesting work also contains the words of 166 hymns which the Wesleys wrote for the Communion Service, pp. 195-249.

28. Cf. Oliver C. Quick, *The Christian Sacraments* (New York: Harper & Bros., 1927); P. T. Forsyth, *Lectures on the Church and Its Sacraments* (London: Longmans, Green & Co., 1927); Robert W. Goodloe, *The Sacraments in Methodism* (Nashville: The Methodist Publishing House, 1953); Olive Wyon, *The Altar Fire: Reflections on the Sacrament of the Eucharist* (London: Student Christian Movement Press, 1954); and Donald M. Baillie, *The Theology of the Sacraments* (New York: Charles Scribner's Sons, 1957).

29. From *The Altar Fire*, by Olive Wyon. 1954, The Westminster Press.

30. *Ibid.*, p. 35.

31. *Ibid.*, p. 37.

32. *Theology of the New Testament*, tr. Kendrick Grobel (New York: Charles Scribner's Sons, 1951), I, 146 ff., especially 147.

33. From the postcommunion Thanksgiving, as found in the Methodist Ritual for the Lord's Supper, *The Book of Worship for Church and Home* (Nashville: The Methodist Publishing House, 1952), p. 380.

CHAPTER VII

1. As found in definitions of the Church such as that quoted in Chap. VI.

2. From *The Teaching Ministry of the Church*, by James D. Smart. Copyright 1954, W. L. Jenkins, The Westminster Press. P. 11.

3. Cf. Randolph Crump Miller, *The Clue to Christian Education* (New York: Charles Scribner's Sons, 1950) and *Biblical Theology and Christian Education* (New York: Charles Scribner's Sons, 1956).

4. Harry C. Munro, *Protestant Nurture: An Introduction to Christian Education* (New York: Prentice-Hall, Inc., 1956), p. 153.

5. The classic statement of this characteristic of modern culture refers to the

"other directed" or "radar type" character structure. See David Riesman (with Nathan Glazer and Reuel Denney), *The Lonely Crowd* (Garden City, N. Y.: Doubleday Anchor Books, 1953), especially pp. 32-48.

6. In psychological terms the nearest approach to this emphasis in learning occurs in the Gestalt insistence that learning actually occurs through the achieving of insight. See George W. Hartmann, *Gestalt Psychology: A Survey of Facts and Principles* (New York: The Ronald Press Company, 1935), pp. 159-201.

7. *The New Being* (New York: Charles Scribner's Sons, 1955), pp. 66-67. Used by permission of the publisher.

8. *Ibid.*, pp. 72-73.

9. Reuel L. Howe, *Man's Need and God's Action* (Greenwich, Conn.: The Seabury Press, 1953), p. 114.

10. *Ibid.*, p. 96. Used by permission of Seabury Press.

11. *Ibid.*, p. 114.

12. *Ibid.*, p. 115.

13. Cf. Lee J. Gable, *Christian Nurture through the Church* (New York: National Council of the Churches of Christ in the U. S. A., 1955), pp. 72-74.

14. See, for example, the Methodist publications, *When the Two-Year Old Comes to Church,* a guide for the leader, and *The Two-Year-Old at Home,* a guide for parents (published by The Methodist Publishing House for the Editorial Division of the Board of Education of The Methodist Church).

15. Cf. Howe, *op. cit.,* especially Chs. vi, vii, and viii.

16. Published by The Methodist Publishing House, Nashville, Tennessee.

17. Cf. Randolph Crump Miller, *The Clue to Christian Education* and *Biblical Theology and Christian Education* for discussions of this process, with illustrations from various Christian beliefs.

18. *Supra,* Chap. VI.

19. Probably the best discussion of the responsibility of the church for dealing with the aged is still *Older People and the Church,* by Paul B. Maves and J. Lennart Cedarleaf (Nashville: Abingdon Press, 1949).

20. *Op. cit.,* especially p. 73.

21. This is a phrase which comes, I believe, from Professor L. Thomas Hopkins of Teachers College, Columbia University.

22. Cf. Miller, *The Clue to Christian Education* and *Biblical Theology and Christian Education.*

23. James D. Smart, *op. cit.,* especially pp. 77-80.

24. *The Gift of Power* (New York: The Macmillan Co., 1955), p. 85. Used by permission of the publisher.

CHAPTER VIII

1. David Riesman (with Nathan Glazer and Reuel Denney), *The Lonely Crowd* (New York: Doubleday Anchor Books, 1953), p. 37. Used by permission of Yale University Press.

2. See, for example, Acts 3:1-8; 8:23-39; 9:17-19; 10:23-48; 16:25-34; 20:7-12, 17-38.

3. Bernard Causton, "No Establishment Probe," *The Christian Century,* LXXII December 21, 1955), 1510.

4. S. R. Slavson, "The Dynamics of Group Process," reprinted from *Character Education in a Democracy,* Ch. iv, in *Readings in Group Work,* ed. Dorothea F. Sullivan (New York: Association Press, 1952), p. 222.

5. "Christian Fellowship and Mental Health," *The Church and Mental Health,* ed. Paul B. Maves (New York: Charles Scribner's Sons, 1953), p. 86. Used by permission of the publisher.

6. *Ibid.,* pp. 86-87.

7. Cf. Estelle A. Alston, "The Leader's Use of Self," in *Readings in Group Work,* pp. 25-38.

8. Reported by Kurt Lewis, Ronald Lippitt, and Ralph K. White in "Patterns of Aggressive Behavior in Experimentally Created 'Social Climates,'" *Readings in Group Work,* Ch. xxv. See also Kurt Lewis, "The Dynamics of Group Action," in *ibid.,* Ch. xxii.

9. Lewis, Lippitt, and White, *op. cit.,* especially p. 359.

10. *Ibid.,* pp. 363-76.

11. Lewin, "The Dynamics of Group Action," *Readings in Group Work,* p. 278.

12. I am greatly indebted to Paul B. Maves, *op. cit.,* for many of the ideas contained in this section.

13. *Ibid.,* p. 95.

14. In order to carry out this plan, there must be a question about which there is some understanding and in which there is interest, and the question must be carefully formulated before it is presented to the group. After a short period of discussion in the subgroups, the findings of each subgroup are presented to the larger group. This plan is especially helpful where members of the group do not know each other, and becoming acquainted is part of the process of group formation. Cf. Mary Alice Douty, *How to Work with Church Groups* (Nashville: Abingdon Press, 1957), pp. 95-98.

15. Administration will be discussed further in Chap. XI.

16. For an interesting brief discussion of resistance to change in the social agency, see Slavson, *op. cit., Readings in Group Work,* pp. 233-34.

17. Robert E. Chiles, "Laymen Study Theology," *The Pastor,* XIX, No. 11 (July, 1956), 30.

18. Robert W. Lynn, "Experiment in Suburbia," *Christianity and Society,* XVIII, No. 2 (Spring, 1953), 21. Used by permission of author and publisher.

19. *Ibid.,* pp. 21, 22.

20. Cf. Harvey Seifert, *Fellowships of Concern: A Manual on the Cell Group Process* (Nashville: Abingdon Press, 1949).

21. Tom Allan, *The Face of My Parish* (London: Student Christian Movement, 1954), pp. 68, 69, 70. Used by permission of the publisher and Harper & Bros.

22. The Protestant Episcopal Church has prepared a manual for guidance of such enterprises. See *A Parish Workshop in Christian Education,* ed. Donald W. Crawford (Greenwich, Conn.: The Seabury Press, 1953).

23. George M. MacLeod, *We Shall Re-Build: The Work of the Iona Community on Mainland and on Island* (Glasgow: The Iona Community [n. d.]).

24. Cf. Elton Trueblood, *Signs of Hope in a Century of Despair* (New York:

Harper & Bros., 1950), pp. 79-80. For further documentation of these various centers, see *Signs of Renewal: The Life of the Lay Institute in Europe* (Geneva: The Department of the Laity, World Council of Churches, Route de Malagnou 17, 1956).

25. Trueblood, *op. cit.*, pp. 99-100.
26. For further information write to W. Jack Lewis, Director, The Christian Faith and Life Community, 2511 Rio Grande, Austin 5, Texas.
27. Cf. William H. Kirkland, "Fellowship and/or Freedom: A Review Article," *The Christian Century*, LXXIV, No. 16 (April 17, 1957), 490-92.
28. This phrase came to me from Professor Charles H. Johnson, lately of the Perkins School of Theology faculty, Dallas, Texas; now of the Garrett Biblical Institute faculty, Evanston, Illinois.

CHAPTER IX

1. H. Richard Niebuhr, *Christ and Culture* (New York: Harper & Bros., 1951), p. 56. Used by permission of the publisher.
2. *Ibid.*, p. 57.
3. *Ibid.*, Ch. ii.
4. *Christian Ethics and Social Policy* (New York: Charles Scribner's Sons, 1946), Ch. iii.
5. *Op. cit.*, Ch. vi.
6. Cf. Paul Tillich, *The New Being* (New York: Charles Scribner's Sons, 1955), sermon no. 2, "The New Being."
7. *Ibid.*, p. 17. Used by permission of Chas. Scribner's Sons.
8. *Ibid.*, pp. 17-18.
9. Cf. Harry C. Munro, *Fellowship Evangelism Through Church Groups* (St. Louis: The Bethany Press, 1951).
10. Chap. IV.
11. "Evangelism—The Mission of the Church to Those Outside Her Life" (Part ii of the volume prepared for the Second Assembly of the World Council of Churches, 1954, and called *The Christian Hope and the Task of the Church*) (New York: Harper & Bros., 1954), p. 59. Used by permission.
12. "The Laity—The Christian in His Vocation" (Part iv of *The Christian Hope and the Task of the Church*), p. 1.
13. Tom Allan, *The Face of My Parish* (London: Student Christian Movement Press, 1954), p. 70. A longer citation will be found *supra*, Chap. VIII.
14. Cf. Ross W. Sanderson, *The Church Serves the Changing City* (New York: Harper & Bros., 1955), Chap. VIII.
15. *Ibid.*, pp. 187-90.
16. Cf. Howard Grimes, "Experiences of an Integrated School," *New South*, XI (February, 1956), 1-5.
17. Cf. Harvey Seifert, *The Church in Community Action* (Nashville: Abingdon Press, 1952).
18. The dissemination of information such as is contained in my article listed in n. 16 is an example.

19. This is a phrase which came to the writer from Dean Merrimon Cuning-gim of the Perkins School of Theology, Southern Methodist University, Dallas, Texas. Cf. "Experiences of an Integrated School," p. 5.
20. Cf. *Evangelism—The Mission of the Church to Those Outside Her Life*, Ch. iii.

CHAPTER X

1. James D. Smart, *The Teaching Ministry of the Church* (Philadelphia: The Westminster Press, 1954), p. 11.
2. Erwin L. Shaver, *Shall Laymen Teach Religion?* (New York: Richard R. Smith, publisher, 1931), p. 25.
3. *Supra*, Chap. VIII.
4. *Your Other Vocation* (New York: Harper & Bros., 1952), p. 107.
5. Published by The Westminster Press (Philadelphia, 1952).
6. Published by Abingdon Press, in twelve volumes (Nashville, various dates).
7. *Systematic Theology*, I (Chicago: The University of Chicago Press, 1951), especially pp. 59-66.
8. I have developed my point of view in this regard more fully in a chapter called "Christianity Is Learned Through Living Encounter with the Bible," in *The Minister and Christian Nurture*, ed. Nathaniel F. Forsyth (Nashville: Abingdon Press, 1957), ch. 6.
9. Published by Charles Scribner's Sons (rev. ed., New York, 1953).
10. Published by Charles Scribner's Sons (New York, 1954).
11. William Hordern, *A Layman's Guide to Protestant Theology* (New York: The Macmillan Company, 1955), p. 186. Used by permission of the publisher. Hordern's book provides an elementary discussion of various theological positions. The "Layman's Theological Library," consisting of twelve volumes under the editorship of Robert McAfee Brown and published by The Westminster Press, is representative of theological books being written for laymen today.
12. Elton Trueblood, *Signs of Hope in a Century of Despair* (New York: Harper & Bros., 1950), Ch. iii.
13. Hordern *op. cit.*, pp. 197-98.
14. *Supra*, Chap. VI.
15. *Supra*, Chap. VI.
16. *Supra*, Chap. VII.
17. *Supra*, Chap. VIII.
18. Practical suggestions of this nature will be found in Price Gwynn's *Leadership Education in the Local Church* (Philadelphia: The Westminster Press, 1952).
19. *Your Other Vocation*, pp. 119-22.
20. *Ibid.*, p. 109.

CHAPTER XI

1. *Supra*, Chap. VIII, IX, and X.
2. One of the facts reported by Dr. Blizzard is that the ministers included

in his survey average spending two-fifths of their working day in administration, one-tenth in work involving organization. The average time for
sermon preparation per day by rural pastors was thirty-four minutes, by
urban pastors, thirty-eight minutes. On the other hand, both average spending sixty-four minutes per day in stenographic work. See Samuel W. Blizzard, "The Minister's Dilemma," *The Christian Century*, LXXIII, No. 17
(April 25, 1956), 508-10.

3. H. Richard Niebuhr, *The Purpose of the Church and Its Ministry* (New
York: Harper & Bros., 1956), pp. 79-94.
4. *Ibid.*, p. 91. Used by permission.
5. Cf. H. Richard Niebuhr, *Christ and Culture* (New York: Harper & Bros.,
1951), Ch. iii.
6. *Ibid.*, Ch. ii.
7. Cf. Albert C. Outler, *Psychotherapy and the Christian Message* (New
York: Harper & Bros., 1954), especially chs. i and vi.
8. *The Purpose of the Church and Its Ministry*, p. 81. Used by permission.
9. Cf. Ross W. Sanderson, *The Church Serves the Changing City* (New York:
Harper & Bros., 1955).

Additional Readings

I. The Nature of the Church

Less advanced:
Brown, William McAfee. *The Significance of the Church.* Philadelphia: The Westminster Press, 1956.
Spike, Robert W. *In But Not of the World: A Notebook of Theology and Practice in the Local Church.* New York: Association Press, 1957.

Somewhat more advanced:
Jenkins, Daniel. *The Strangeness of the Church.* Garden City, New York: Doubleday & Co., 1955.
Niebuhr, H. Richard (in collaboration with Daniel Day Williams and James M. Gustafson). *The Purpose of the Church and Its Ministry.* New York: Harper & Bros., 1956.

More advanced:
Brunner, Emil. *The Misunderstanding of the Church.* Philadelphia: The Westminster Press, 1953.
Dillistone, F. W. *The Structure of the Divine Society.* Philadelphia: The Westminster Press, 1951.
Flew, R. Newton, ed. *The Nature of the Church: Papers Presented to the Theological Commission Appointed by the Continuation Committee of the World Conference on Faith and Order.* New York: Harper & Bros., 1952.
Nelson, J. Robert. *The Realm of Redemption.* Greenwich, Conn.: The Seabury Press, 1951.
Newbigin, Lesslie. *The Household of God.* New York: Friendship Press, 1954.
Niebuhr, H. Richard and Daniel D. Williams, eds. *The Ministry in Historical Perspectives.* New York: Harper & Bros., 1956.
Thornton, L. S. *The Common Life in the Body of Christ.* Westminster: Dacre Press, 1941.

II. Christian Vocation
Forrester, W. R. *Christian Vocation: Studies in Faith and Work.* London: Lutterworth Press, 1951.

Nelson, John Oliver, ed. *Work and Vocation: A Christian Discussion.* New York: Harper & Bros., 1954.

Richardson, Alan. *The Biblical Doctrine of Work: Ecumenical Biblical Studies No. 1.* London: Student Christian Movement Press, 1952.

World Council of Churches. *The Laity—The Christian in His Vocation.* Part iv of *The Christian Hope and the Task of the Church.* New York: Harper & Bros., 1954.

III. Worship

Bishop, John. *Methodist Worship.* London: The Epworth Press, 1950.

Hedley, George. *Christian Worship.* New York: The Macmillan Company, 1953.

Jones, Ilion T. *A Historical Approach to Evangelical Worship.* Nashville: Abingdon Press, 1954.

Maxwell, William D. *An Outline of Christian Worship.* New York: Oxford University Press, 1936, 1955.

Rattenbury, J. Ernest. *The Eucharistic Hymns of John and Charles Wesley.* London: The Epworth Press, 1949.

————. *Vital Elements of Public Worship.* London: The Epworth Press, 1936, 1954.

Shepherd, Massey. *The Worship of the Church.* Greenwich, Conn.: The Seabury Press, 1952.

Underhill, Evelyn. *Worship.* New York: Harper & Bros., 1936, 1957.

IV. Christian Nurture

Forsyth, Nathaniel F., ed. *The Minister and Christian Nurture.* Nashville: Abingdon Press, 1957.

Gable, Lee J. *Christian Nurture Through the Church.* New York: National Council of the Churches of Christ in the U.S.A., 1955.

Howe, Reuel. *Man's Need and God's Action.* Greenwich, Conn.: The Seabury Press, 1953.

Miller, Randolph Crump. *Biblical Theology and Christian Education.* New York: Charles Scribner's Sons, 1956.

————. *The Clue to Christian Education.* New York: Charles Scribner's Sons, 1950.

————. *Education for Christian Living.* New York: Prentice-Hall, Inc., 1956.

Munro, Harry C. *Protestant Nurture: An Introduction to Christian Education.* New York: Prentice-Hall, Inc., 1956.

Sherrill, Lewis J. *The Gift of Power.* New York: The Macmillan Co., 1955.

Smart, James D. *The Teaching Ministry of the Church.* Philadelphia: The Westminster Press, 1954.

Wyckoff, D. Campbell. *The Task of Christian Education.* Philadelphia: The Westminster Press, 1955.

V. Group Life

Casteel, John L., ed. *Spiritual Renewal Through Personal Groups.* New York: Association Press, 1957.

Douglass, Paul F. *The Group Workshop Way in the Church.* New York: Association Press, 1956.

Douty, Mary Alice. *How to Work with Church Groups.* Nashville: Abingdon Press, 1957.

Maves, Paul B., ed. *The Church and Mental Health.* New York: Charles Scribner's Sons, 1953.

Sullivan, Dorothea F., ed. *Readings in Group Work.* New York: Association Press, 1952.

Trueblood, Elton. *Signs of Hope in a Century of Despair.* New York: Harper & Bros., 1950.

VI. Outreach

Allan, Tom. *The Face of My Parish.* London: Student Christian Movement Press, 1954.

Sanderson, Ross W. *The Church Serves the Changing City.* New York: Harper & Bros., 1955.

Seifert, Harvey. *The Church in Community Action.* Nashville: Abingdon Press, 1952.

World Council of Churches. *Evangelism—The Mission of the Church to Those Outside Her Life* (Part ii) and *The Laity—The Christian in His Vocation* (Part iv), in *The Christian Hope and the Task of the Church.* New York: Harper & Bros., 1954.

VII. Leadership

Gwynn, Price. *Leadership Education in the Local Church.* Philadelphia: The Westminster Press, 1952.

Smart, James D. *The Teaching Ministry of the Church.* Philadelphia: The Westminster Press, 1952.

Trueblood, Elton. *Your Other Vocation.* New York: Harper & Bros., 1952.

VIII. Administration

See books listed under *Leadership* and *Group Life*

Gable, Lee J. *Christian Nurture Through the Church* (New York: National Council of the Churches of Christ in the U.S.A., 1955). Especially chs. iv and v which summarize an unpublished doctoral dissertation by William D. Case, "A Democratic Conception of the Administration of a Local Church," New York: Teachers College, Columbia University, 1953.

Index of Scripture References

Index of Subjects

Church school, 95-103, 116-17
Church of South India, 87
"Church work," 64
Class churches, 56
Class meeting, 107, 108, 120
Clericalism, 16
Commitment, 60, 148
Committees, 165
Community, 29; of faith, 17; of persons, 27, 28, 35. See also Koinonia
Conditioning, 91-92
Confirmation, 31, 84-85, 100, 104
Congregational polity, 25, 33
Conversion, 60, 104
Curriculum, 103-4

Dedication, 60
Democracy, 40-42, 113
Denney, Reuel, 176
Dewey, John, 91, 155
Didachē, 105
Dillenberger, John, 144
Dillistone, F. W., 23, 28, 31, 32
Directors of Christian Education, 65, 165-66
Disciples of Christ, 80
Dix, Gregory, 74
"Drama of redemption," 36

East Harlem Protestant Parish, 132-33
Ecumenical Institute (Boissey), 45, 121
Ecumenical institutes, 150
Ecumenical movement, 136-37
Ekklēsia, 38-39, 65
Election, 38-39
Encounter, 93-95, 103, 104-5, 161-62
Ethics, 145
Eucharist. See Lord's Supper
Evangelical academies, 121
Evangelism, 66-67, 119, 129-31
Extension of the Incarnation, 15

Faith, 31 ff.
Family, 26, 29, 31-32, 51-52, 54, 99, 102-3, 164
Fellowship. See Koinonia
Filson, Floyd V., 143
First Methodist Church, Jacksonville, Tex., 98

First Methodist Church, Lubbock, Tex., 97
Forgiveness, 126
Forrester, W. R., 63
Freedom, 28, 122, 158

God: acceptance, 58, 84 ff.; activity of, 14, 18, 31, 34, 36, 54; call of, 60 ff.; chooses us, 38; forgiveness, 29-30, 31; incarnation of, 22, 27, 41, 148; love of, 125; "object" of service, 35, 59-60, 68, 73 ff.; "object" of worship, 72 ff., 87-88; power of, 17; relation to human selves, 26, 55, 59, 113, 167; Trinitarian belief, 161
Golden Age clubs, 102
Grace, 32, 58
Graham, Billy, 108
Group dynamics, 156. See also Groups
Groups, 107 ff., 149; church, 111-12, 115-22; "in-group, out-group," 123; nature of, 110-12, 115-16, 123; neighborhood, 120; new church, 118-21; therapeutic, 119-20; types, 116-18

Hall, G. Stanley, 101
Hardin, Grady, 120
Highland Park Methodist Church, Dallas, Tex., 97
History, 22
Holy Club, 57
Holy Communion. See Lord's Supper
Holy Spirit, 15, 22, 35, 41-42, 47, 49, 50-51, 53, 55, 57, 66, 79, 85-87, 105, 110, 144, 150, 153, 157, 160, 161-62, 167
Hordern, William, 145
Hosea, 17
Housman, A. E., 36
Howe, Reuel, 27, 57, 94-95
Humanitarianism, 126

"I-It," 158-59
"I-Thou," 26, 90, 95, 158-59
Incarnation, 22, 27, 41, 148
Individualism, 23-25